S R Ranganathan

Birth Centenary Literature

S R Ranganathan
Birth Centenary Literature

Sewa Singh

Ess Ess Publications

4837/24, ANSARI ROAD, DARYA GANJ
NEW DELHI - 110002
Phone : 3260807

First Published 1995

Rs. Ess Ess
Rs.400/-

ISBN - 81-7000-180-3

Published by:

Ess Ess Publications
4837/24, Ansari Road, Daryaganj,
New Delhi - 110002.

Typeset at
Academy of Computer Studies
Bg-1/42, Paschim Vihar
New Delhi - 110063
Phone - 558 0312

CONTENTS

PREFACE

From time to time Dr S R Ranganathan has been a center of attention not only in his own country but in the world outside as well. He became a central figure by producing a new system of library classification called Colon Classification, and the theory of classification which he developed for its sustenance he got the attention of the library world by publishing his seminal work on Five Laws of Library Science. At the international conferences particularly from Dorking Conference, he always attracted gatherings for his unique and novel ideas.

At the age of 70 a two volume festschrift publication was presented to him, and the second volume was a bibliography of the works by and on Ranganathan.

After living a full life of 80 years (about 50 years of professional life) he breathed his last on 27 September 1972. This otherwise sad event brought out the publication of a large number of Special Issues of various professional journals in India and abroad paying rich tributes to the departed soul, and eulogising his contribution that enriched library and information science literature.

The Indian Library Association in collaboration with other bodies organised an International Conference on the philosophy and relevance of Dr S R Ranganathan's contribution, in November 1985 in New Delhi. The delegates at the Conference, foreign and Indian, discussed the philosophy behind his work, the relevance of his contribution in today's situation. This Conference also produced a good number of literature on and about Ranganathan. It was on this occasion that a bibliography on Ranganathan was complied on behalf of the National Social Science Documentation Centre (NASSDOC), and was released and distributed among the participants of the Conference.

Meanwhile, articles, books, and other research work continued to be published on Ranganathan at some of the library and information science schools in India and abroad. Some of them also prepared Ph D theses on the works and contribution of Ranganathan both in India and abroad. Students of Master in Library and Information Science degree courses ventured to produce dissertations on Ranganathan's contribution, and some of them even compiled bibliographies of literature published on him restricting them to some periods.

Another important, probably the most important event of this century associated with S R Ranganathan was his Birth Centenary year 1992. The Indian Library Association had already approached the IFLA to organise its Annual Conference in India to mark the Birth Centenary of the great librarian and library educator. Came 1991, and the Birth Centenary celebrations of this world renowned librarian were triggered off with the holding of the Third International Conference on Informetrics in August 1991 at Bangalore. Informetrics has its roots in 'Librametry', a term Ranganathan coined way back in 1948. And in 1992, a spurt of activities started to celebrate the Birth Centenary in a variety of ways and befitting manner. Library and Information Science schools, library associations, and other bodies organised various seminars, lectures, books and photograph exhibitions, talks, stamp release, bust installation, etc. Among others, Madras Library Association (MALA) has been quite active only to express its gratitude to him that it was established by none other than Ranganathan himself in 1928. MALA, in collaboration with the Institute of Information Studies, and the Department of Library & Information Science, University of Madras, organised the Second International Conference of ISKO (Germany) in August 1992 at Madras. The Indian Library Association organised its 38th All India Library Conference in his memory at Bhubaneswar, and the Volume of seminar papers were dedicated to Ranganathan as a mark of tribute. Similarly, the Indian Association of Special Libraries and Information Centres (IASLIC) also organised its National Seminar at the Annamalai University, Annamalainagar in December 1992. At this occasion a book dedicated to the luminaries of the library profession including Ranganathan was also released.

The Birth Centenary Year produced a plethora of library and information literature in the form of articles, books, monographs, souvenirs, special numbers of the professional and non professional journals, and even some news papers published special features on Ranganathan.

The spill over of the publication of literature on and about the man continued in 1993 and even upto the first quarter of 1994, so that some books and special numbers of some periodicals were published in 1993; while a couple of seminars and talks were organised in the first half of 1994 resulting in more literature on Ranganathan.

The premier publication, among all these, which stands shoulders above, is obviously the autobiography of Ranganathan:

A Librarian looks back, which was serailised in the *Herald of Library Science* since the days of its first volume in 1962.

In view of the steady growth of literature during the Birth Centenary celebrations, it was decided to gather all the literature produced during the international event. But as the celebrations continued for more than a year, the exercise of gathering the relevant material continued, and given a stop with the holding of a Seminar on Ranganathan by the Punjab Library Association in April 1994.

The aim of this bibliographical complication therefore has been to identify and arrange together all the relevant materials on and about the life, works, impact of his contribution on librarianship, comparative librarianship, and other fields of library and information science from such first hand sources as the Special Numbers of various journals, books and edited books for the occasion on the great master, few articles of relevace from the 58th IFLA General Conference, a couple of relevant articles from the Second International ISKO Conference, foreign journals, Souvenirs, and other sources. From the Special Numbers on Ranganathan all the material has not been included, as some of it was of general nature, while others did not discuss the ideas of Ranganathan. Hence it may seem that the compilation is less than complete. This may also seem true as the material published on him during these years in languages other than English could also not be covered. Nor have been included the dissertations and Ph D theses prepared by the students.

However, effort has been made to dig out the published material from all the possible sources and make it a further source of information on the Birth Centenary literature. A total of 412 entries have been collected and given a subject arrangement beginning with the Autobiography, Biography / Life and Work, Comparative Biography, Letters, Honours and Awards, Conferences held on him, Ranganathan and Professional Associations, Impact on International / World Librarianship, Contribution to the various aspects of librarianship, and so on. About a dozen citations have also been included in the Supplement. As was expected, the Birth Centenary Year, 1992, published maximum literature (i.e, 255 items), followed by 105 items in 1993, and 26 in 1994. The areas which attracted the attention of the contributors are the general explanatory nature of writings on the life and works of Ranganathan, interpretation and relevance of his contribution to Five Laws and other fields of library and information science. Of course, library classification still remains the most sought after area for the scholars to venture in. However, other equally important areas such as cataloguing and indexing, library management, reference and information services, documentation services, information retrieval, etc, have not got much attention in the form of published literature during the period of coverage.

This spurt of literature published on Dr. S R Ranganathan, holding of international conferences, seminars, lectures, etc during the Birth Centenary celebrations which attracted the attention of all the world's library and information professionals has helped in ushering a new age in this new information society. We, who happen to be his fellow countrymen must seize the opportunity to build a new image of the profession when the libraries and information centres are being gradually computerised. We must not only preach the high ideals and expectations cherished by Ranganathan but must also emulate and set the example for the new generations of library and information scientists so that they could become the torch bearers of tomorrow.

Amritsar
August 12, 1994.

Sewa Singh

ABBREVIATIONS OF JOURNALS INDEXED

AGLIS Jl	AGLIS Journal
Ann Lib Sci & Docum	Annals of Library science and documentation
Aryan Heritage	Aryan Heritage
Bhavan's Jl	Bhavan's Journal
Bull d' info de 1' Asso des Biblio Franeais	Bulletin d' informations de 1' Association des biblio the carires Francais
Boll AIB	Bolletino AIB
Ciencia da Inf	Ciencia da Information
CLA Souvenir	Chandigarh Librarians Association Souvenir
CLIS Observer	CLIS Observer
College Res News	College and Research Libraries News
College Lib	College Libraries
DESIDOC Bull	DESIDOC Bulletin of Information Technology
DRTC Annual Semi	DRTC Annual Seminar
Focus on Int & Comp Libnship	Focus on International and Comparative Librarianship
Frontline	Frontline
Her Lib Sci	Herald of Library Science

Hindu	The Hindu (Madras)
IASLIC Bull	Indian Association of Special Libraries and Information Centres Bulletin
IJILIS	Indian Journal of Information, Library and Society
IJILIS News	Indian Journal of Information, Library and Society Newsletter
ILA Bull	Indian Library Association Bulletin
Ind Bk Chronicle	Indian Book Chronicle
Ind Bk Industry	Indian Book Industry
Inf Docum Problems	Information Documentation Problems
Inf Management Rep	Information Management Report
INICAE	International Information Communication and Education
Int Cat & Bib Control	International Cataloguing and Biblio graphical Control
Int Classif	International Classification
Int Lib Move	International Library Movement
IPLA Souvenir	Indian Public Library Association Souvenir
Jl Lib & Inf Sci	Journal of Library and Information Science
Kirjastotiedega	Kirjastotiedega
Libri	Libri: International Library Review

Lib Her	Library Herald
Lib Hist Rev	Library History Review
Lib Sci slant Docum & Inf Std	Library Science with a slant to Documentation and Information Studies
Lib Times Int	Library Times International
Lib Today	Library Today
Luck Libn	Lucknow Librarian
NISSAT Newsletter	NISSAT Newsletter
Par Biblio	Par Biblioteka
Rilisar Bull	Ranganathan Institute of Library and Information Science and Applied Research Bulletin
Souvenir of PLA	Souvenir of Punjab Library Association
Soviet Bibl	Soviet Bibliotheca
T P & D Eorum Series	T P & S Eorum Series
Technalities	Technalities
Timeless Fellowship	Timeless Fellowship
Univ News	University News

ABBREVIATIONS AND THEIR EXPLANATIONS

CC	Colon Classification 7th Edition : Some perspectives, Edited by MP Satija, New Delhi: Sterling Publishers, 1993, xx, 220 p.
CPT	Current problems and trends in library and information services: Prof K S Deshpande festschrift volume, Edited by H A Khan and S R Ijari, Varanasi: Indian Bibliographical Centre, 1990, iii, 370p.
DL	Dynamics of librarianship; felicitation to luminaries in the profession-Birth Centenary publication of Dr S R Ranganathan, Annamalainagar: Department of Library and Information Science, Annamalai University, 1992, x, 327+14p.
DLIS	Dimensions of library and information science: Kaula festschrift, Edited by V Venkatappaiah, et al, New Delhi: Concept Publishing Company, 1990, 690p.
ILS	Institute of Library Science, Hyderabad, Souvenir, Edited by S Sudarshan Rao, Hyderabad: Institute of Library Science, 1991, various unnnumbered pages.
LIS	Library and Information science: Trends and challenges: Essays in honour of Professor S S Agrawal, Edited by A Tejomurty and S Kumar, New Delhi: Indus Publishing Company, 1993, 192p.
PP	Petits petals: A tribute to S R Ranganathan, Edited by K Navalani and M P Satija, New Delhi: A B C Publishing House, 1993, xiv,150p.
RAT	Dr. S R Ranganathan: A tribute (on the occasion of his Centenary celebration). Calcutta: The National Library, 1993, vii, 57p.

RAW	S R Ranganathan and the West, Edited by R N Sharma, New Delhi: Sterling Publishers, 1992, xvii,179p.
RMM	Seminar of Ranganathan: Man and mission, by Punjab Library Association, held at the Punjab University, Patiala, from April 29-30, 1994, Seminar papers, Patiala: Punjab Library Association,1994, iv,129p.
SRR	S R Ranaganathan, 1892-1972, Edited by Edward Dudley, New Delhi: Ess Ess Publications, 1992, 39 p (First Indian Reprint; originally published by the Library Association, London, 1973).
ULI	University libraries in India; 1980s and beyond: Essays in honour of Prof. T P Saxena, New Delhi: Medallion Press, 1991, viii, 290p.

OTHER BOOKS BY THE SAME AUTHOR

Directory of Librarians & Libraries of Punjab (New Delhi : Anmol Publications, 1995)

Colon Classification Practice (Jalandhar : ABS Publishers, 1995)

Indian Library and information Science Literature, 1990-1991 (New Delhi : Concept Publishing Company, 1994)

Handbook of College Libraries : Problems, Development, etc ... (New Delhi: Beacon Books, 1994)

Colon Classification; A Select Bibliography (New Delhi : Ess Ess Publications, 1992)

Indian Library and Information Science Literature, 1986-1989 (New Delhi : Ess Ess Publications, 1991)

Practical Manual of Colon Classification, Ed-7 (Bombay : JAICO, 1990)

Indian Library Literature, 1981-1985; an Annotated Bibliography (New Delhi : Ess Ess Publications, 1988)

Librarianship and Library Science Education : Essays in honour of Dr J S Sharma, (New Delhi : Ess Ess Publications, 1988)

Indian Library Literature, 1971-1980; an Annotated Bibliographic Guide (New Delhi : Today & Tomorrow's Publishers, 1986)

Reference Service in Academic Libraries (New Delhi : Ess Ess Publications, 1986)

ACKNOWLEDGMENTS

In preparing this work of the Birth Centenary Literature of Dr. S R Ranganathan, I have depended upon a large number of primary sources. I wish to record my sincere thanks to all those authors whose materials I have freely used in this compilation. Besides, many friends and well wishers, editors of journals, etc have cared to supply me the necessary material on Dr. S.R. Ranganathan, without whose help this work would not have been complete. I would like to record my gratitude to all of them. I may mention the names of Ms. Kalpana Dasgupta, Librarian, National Library, Calcutta; P.N Santhanagopal, Public Relations Officer, Bhartiya Vidya Bhavan, Bombay; B. L. Basu, Editor, College Libraries; Sh Narendra Lahkar, Reader, Dept of Library and Information Science, Gauhati University; Mr S. K. Ghai of Sterling Publishers; Sh Praveen Mittal, Director, B R Publishing Corporation; Proprietor, Mohanvalli Publications, Madras; late Sh S K Sethi, Ess Ess Publications, New Delhi; Dr. (Mrs) M Suriya, Head, Dept of Library and Information Science, Annamalai University; Sh Somnath Raha of West Bengal College Librarians Association; Sh G L Trehan of Chandigarh; Dr B B Shukla, Editor, IJILIS, Cuttack; Editors of Desidoc Bulletin; Dr Suseela Kumar, President, Madras Library Association; Sh G S Dhillon of CSIO, Chandigarh; Sh D R Kalia, Editor, CLIS Observer.

I am thankful to my wife, Narinder Kaur, and children Serebdeep, Amardeep and Masha Sondeep for their patience during its compilation.

Part - I

AUTOBIOGRAPHY

LIFE AND WORK, ETC

AUTOBIOGRAPHY

RANGANATHAN, S R 1

A librarian looks back: An autobiography of Dr S R Ranganathan, appended with an evaluation of his life and work, by P N Kaula, New Delhi: A B C Publishing House, 1992. (Kaula Series in Library Science, 11). xiv, 485 p, 34 photographs.

This autobiography of the great Indian library scientist, Dr S R Ranganathan has been divided into two parts. Part A gives Ranganathan's professional career and his days of struggle, learning, work, experiments etc. with the Library of the University of Madras. This part starts with the background of his application to the post of the University Librarian in July, 1923 and ends describing the last days of his association with the University. Part B describes Ranganathan's activities with different professional associations and conferences with special reference to the Madras Library Association and the Indian Library Association. This part goes up to the year 1963. Evaluates Ranganathan's contribution in the last Part prepared by Kaula (Part C). The autobiography was serialised by Ranganathan under the heading 'A Librarian Looks Back' in the quarterly journal *Herald of Library Science* (1962-1972).

BIOGRAPHY. LIFE AND WORK

ADELMAN, JEAN S 2

A memory of S R Ranganathan, *DL*, 1-2.

Remembers the author's contact with Ranganathan, with particular references to his contribution of Five Laws of Library Science and their relevance. States how the author in few weeks contact with Ranganathan continues to inform some of the attitudes and actions as a librarian to this day.

AGARWAL, S C 3

He ushered a new era...., In *Souvenir* of CLA, 1992.

Relates Ranganathan's contribution, achievements, honours and awards he got in India and abroad including the title of Padam Shri, and honour of National Professor of Library Science in India. Pays rich tributes to this glittering personality in his Birth Centenary Year.

AHLUWALIA, J K 4

Legacy of Dr S R Ranganathan, *Ann Lib Sc & Docum* 39 (2) June 1992: i.

Writes in this Editorial of this Special Number of this old journal, as a homage, about the contribution of Dr Ranganathan to the field of library and information science. States that as a prolific writer, as a teacher he had few peers, and is called 'Messiah of Library World' . Mentions about his association with Indian National Scientific Documentation Centre (INSDOC) during its formative years, and also as the founder Editor of the *Annals of Library Science*, as it was then called.

ARORA, MADHURI 5

Father of Library Science: Dr Ranganathan, *Aryan Heritage* 11(97) Dec 1992: 22-23.

Deals with Ranganathan's birth, brief life account, awards, degrees, honours etc. which he received during his life time. Describes his contribution to Librarianship. States that he made the foundation of Library and Information Science education in India and that we are following the same pattern even now.

ATANASIU, P and THEODORE, V 6

The anatomy of Shiyali Ramamrita Ranganathan's anniversary, *Inf Docum Problems* (Romania) 26 (2) 1992: 106-111.

Describes the Centenary celebrations of Dr S R Ranganathan, whose writings created a new age of thinking in librarianship. Also describes Ranganathan's research in knowledge organisation and Colon Classification for which he is more known.

BALRAM KAUR 7

Guiding light to the librarians, In *Souvenir* of CLA, 1992.

Remembers Ranganathan's contribution, his dedication, devotion, humility, austerity, and philanthropy, particularly in creating a Professorship in Library Science at the University of Madras and also the Sarada Ranganathan Endowment for Library Science (Bangalore) which is continuing with his good work. Pays rich tributes to him in the Birth Centenary year.

BANKAPUR, M B 8

Dr S R Ranganathan - a live specimen of librarianship, *IJILIS* 5(3-4) July-Dec 1992: 253-257.

Describes Ranganathan as an intellectual elite who rose from humble origin. Gives account of his life and works which led to the 'Age of Ranganathan'. Describes his qualities as a man. Makes an assessment of his work in the field of librarianship. Describes Ranganathan as the perfect representative of the 20th century who accomplished something that no one else did at the time.

BERA, CHITTARANJAN 9

Dr S R Ranganathan: A great teacher and organiser of Library Science, *College Lib* 8 (1-2) 1992: 26-27.

Pays tribute to Ranganathan as a great teacher of library science. Concludes that we the Indian workers in library and information filed should practice Ranganathan's ideas of library service which will raise and strengthen the status and importance of library service in modern society.

BHARGAVA, G D 10

Dr S R Ranganathan - My teacher and mentor, *PP*, 109-115

Describes Ranganathan as a great man who opined that library professional should not live on profession but for it. Recaptulates author's initiation in the library profession as Ranganathan's student, his association and meetings with Ranganathan and first hand study of Ranganathan as a teacher who was a hard task master, and a professional seer par excellence.

BHATIA, JASPAL KAUR 11

Our godfather, In *Souvenir* of CLA, 1992.

States that due to his unique contribution to the field of librarianship Ranganathan will be remembered in the days to come as a benefactor and our godfather. Pays rich tributes to him for intiating the library movement in India as well as for establishing a large number of libraries and making people realise the importance and usefulness of these temples of knowledge.

BHATIA, K K AND GUPTA, S P 12

In the footsteps of the great master: Some innovative information service at CRRI, *AGLIS Jl* 9,1993 (Abstract only).

Describes the various information services being given at the Central Road Research Institute, New Delhi such as 'Emerging Technologies', 'Global Developments', 'Pragmatic Development', Emerging Terminology', and so on in the footsteps of the great master, Ranganathan. Concludes that these innovations have helped the users of the library.

BOSE, ANINDYA 13

Ranganathan: An impressionistic view, *RAW*, 170-173.

Discusses about the author's brief meetings with Ranganathan. Relates the interesting character traits which impressed the author. Lauds the monumental contribution of Ranganathan to the field of librarianship. Concludes that his work and contribution impressed the author more than Ranganathan as a person. Mentions further that we need a Ranganathan at the moment to integrate the relevant segments of information science into library science so that the discipline can move forward and remain viable.

CHOPRA, H R 14

Dr S R Ranganathan : Father of library movement in India, In *Souvenir* of CLA, 1992.

Discusses about Ranganathan's Five Laws, Colon Classification, Classified Catalogue Code, and other contributions as a librarian and library and information science teacher. Mentions his association with professional bodies at national and international level such as ILA, FID, IFLA, UNESCO, etc. Mentions about the awards he received in India and abroad. States that by holding the 58th Conference of IFLA at New Delhi from 30th August to 5th September, 1992, the world of librarianship has paid rich tributes to him in his Birth Centenary year.

CHOPRA, RAJINDER 15

Still remains an ideal for me, in *Souvenir* of CLA, 1992.

Pays tributes to Ranganathan who loved his students, and was ideal for many including the author. Recaptulates some of the fine memories as a student of Ranganathan who was a disciplinarian but also took personal interest in his students. States that he had complete devotion and dedication to librarianship. Mentions about his other qualities of simplicity wearing dhoti and kurta but deeply plunged in the study of his subject.

DAHLBERG, I 16

Editorial: Ethics and Knowledge organization in memory of Dr S R Ranganathan in his centenial year, *Int Classif* 19(1) 1992 : 1-2.

Pays tribute to Ranganathan by bringing out this Special Number of *International Classification*. Includes four articles on and about Ranganathan's contribution. Gives a brief account about his life and hard work he used to do for the profession. Outlines some of his qualities in relation to ethics.

DASGUPTA, KALPANA 17

Introduction, *RAT*, v-vi.

States that this compilation, *S R Ranganathan: A Tribute*, has been prepared with the sole idea of paying tribute to the doyen of library and information science from general staff members of the National Library (of India), Calcutta. Gives the resume of the ten articles included in the compilation on Ranganathan's different contributions to the field of library and information science.

DESHPANDE, V W 18

Dr S R RANGANATHAN, librarian extraordinary, *Bhavan's Journal* 39 (20) May 31,1993 : 26-27

Recounts some of the most interesting but full of advise, anecdotes from the life of Ranaganathan as librarian, and the service he rendered to his users, big and small, rich and poor alike. Pays tribute to him on the occasion of his Birth Centenary year celebrated in 1992 all over the world of librarianship.

Dr S R RANGANTHAN - a sketch, *Bhavan's journal* 39 (20) May 31,1993: 18-19. 19

Provides a brief and sketchy picture of Ranganathan's birth, achievements and contributions to the field of libraries and librarianship. Describe that his sole aim was to bring alive the First Law of Library Science, i.e."Books are for Use". Pays tribute to the great master.

Dr S R RANAGANTHAN : A tribute (on the occasion of his Centenary celebrations), Calcutta: The National Library, 1993. vii, 57p. 20

Brought out as a tribute to the great master, S R Ranganathan on the occasion of his Centenary Celebrations by the staff members of the National Library. Includes ten articles contributed by the staff of the National Library of

India on different aspects of library and information science and tries to highlight Ranaganathan's contribution, image of his life and work in the field of libraries and librarianship.

DUDLEY, EDWARD, *Ed* 21

S R Ranaganthan, 1892 - 1972, New Delhi: Ess Ess Publications, 1992. 39p. (First Indian Reprint; Originally published by the Library Association, London, 1973).

This Indian reprint brought out on the occasion of the Birth Centenary celebration of Ranganathan includes six valuable papers contributed by his admirers and friends in England who applied Ranganathan's ideas in classification, documentation and indexing, laws of library science, etc. to the British librarianship successfully.

FLYING LIBRARIAN; first and the only, 22

In *Souvenir* of CLA, 1992.

Mentions some of the first achievements of S R Ranganathan both at the national and international level such as establishment of MALA, first Public Library Act, UGC Committee on Library affairs, first full time University Librarian of the Madras University, first Librarian to be awarded Padamshri, and so on at the national level. At the international level first librarian to tour Europe and USA, first to attend IFLA, Chairman of the FID Committee, Vice President of FID, and so on.

GARFIELD, EUGENE 23

A tribute to Ranganathan, the father of Indian library science, *RAW*, 121-128.

Discusses life and works of Ranaganathan. Mentions his objections to the prevailing classification systems and as a result gave the new classification system called *Colon Classification*. Describes his contribution to cataloguing and other fields also, such as library science education, public libraries. Mentions that his contributions were acknowledged many times over, both in India and abroad. Pays tribute to the great man on the occasion of his Birth Centenary celebration.

GAURI, KUL B 24

Language as ritual in the library discourse of Ranganathan, *RAW*, 112-120.

Examines the nature of the Ranganathan's style and discourse which is derived and based on a specific category of Hindu scriptures and literature. States that his style reflects the use of the language as ritual derived from his cultural moorings. Mentions some of the unique features of Ranganathan's discourse such as the creation and use of metaphors, expanding the use of words to express and shape his thinking and writing.

GIAN SINGH 25

He was an institution in himself, In *Souvenir* of CLA, 1992.

States that through his works and deeds, Ranganathan carved out for himself a permanent niche in the library movement. Mentions that he dealt with all aspects of the library, and his writings will act as the guidelines for the generations to come. Pays tributes to him as a genius, held in high esteem.

GIRJA KUMAR 26

Creativity in the thought of Dr S R Ranganathan, *Ann Lib Sc & Docum* 39(2) June 1992: 46-51.

Points out Ranganathan's religious and cultural background. Describes him as a pragmatist, and the other side of his personalty as a believer in occult philosophy. Discusses impact of mysticism on him and his work, impact of Indian religious scriptures on his writings. Gives the spirit of the library as envisaged by Ranganathan. Draws analogies and three planes of work. Mentions about his intellectual essence, Ekavakyata principle, holistic principle. Describe his intellection, creativity, intuition, etc.

GIRJA KUMAR 27

Creatively in the thought of Dr S R Ranganthan, *CLIS Observer* 9 (1-2) Jan-June 1992: 25-32.

Discusses impact of religion, occult, mysticism, and Indian scriptures on Ranganthan. Mentions the spirit of the library which he enjoyed and practised. Discusses his freedom of intellect and Ekvakyata principle of unity of ideas, holistic principle, intellection, and creativity in detail.

GIRJA KUMAR 28

Indian roots of Dr S R Ranganathan's thought, *Jl of Lib & Inf Sc* 17 (1) June 1992: 1-16.

Argues that the mainsprings of Ranganathan's thought are derived from his oriental origins. Points out that some people say that his many ideas had emerged from his spirtual background. Mentions that he had great moral sense due to his Brahmanic background. Describes the place of intuition, creativity, imagination and mysticism in the development of his thought.

GIRJA KUMAR 29

The library scientist: Remembering S R Ranganathan, *Frontline* 9 (17) Aug 15-28, 1992: 58-60.

Describes Ranaganathan as quintessential intellectual at par with such scientists as Sir C V Raman and Charles Darwin. Explains his seminal contribution to the field of library and information science such as *Colon Classification*, Five Laws of Library Science, theory of classification, and *Prolegomena*, *Classified Catalogue Code*, establishment of Documentation Research and Training Centre, Bangalore. :arrates his tormentoes at the University of Madras.

GIRJA KUMAR 30

Prince amongst librarians, *The Times of India*, August 9,1992.

Discusses brief sketch of life and contribution of Dr S R Ranganathan who is considered as the prince amongst librarians. Reflects Ranganathan's devotion to librarianship with intellectual stimula and hard work coupled with creativity, mysticism, and intuition.

GIRJA KUMAR 31

Relevance of Ranganathan, *CLIS Observer* 8 (3-4) July-Dec 1991: 43-48.

Examines critically the relevance of Ranganathan's contributions. Delineates their strength and limitations in the context of recrnt developments in the field of library and information science. States that his basic contributions need to be reassessed to make them relevant to the present day needs.

GIRJA KUMAR 32

S R Ranganathan: An intellectual biography, New Delhi: Har-Anand Publications, 1992. 327p.

Divided into two parts, Part I deals with Ranganathan as 'The man' giving account of his life in his social milieu, his activities and achievements. In Part II the author makes an assessment of Ranganathan's work personality as 'The Intellect'. Evaluates Ranganathan's fundamental laws and canons, application of scientific method, faceted classification, postulational approach and mnemonics, etc. Presents his psyco-analytico study and social environment in which he worked. Deals with Ranganathan's study system, the holistic approach, and his creativity.

GIRJA KUMAR 33

S R Ranganathan; an intellectual par excellence, In G L Trehan and Girja Kumar: *Ranganthan Birth Centenary Monograph*, Chandigarh: Chandigarh Library Study Circle, 1993, pp 29-35.

Discusses Ranganathan's birth, his contribution which went on to transform beyond recognition what has today emerged as the discipline of library and information science. Describes him as an intellectual par excellence who had no hesitation in comparing him with such stalwarts as Charles Darwin and Sir C V Raman. Mentions that in this field all his contributions flowed from one single idea - Five Laws of Library Science.

GOPINATH, M A 34

Ranganathan's perspectives and achievements: Guest Editorial, *Lib Sci slant Docum & Inf Std* 29 (3) Sept 1992: i-iv.

States that Ranganathan lived through a period of renaissance where libraries had a primary objective of preservation which he enlarged. Emphasises that Ranganathan's perspective are to be analysed in this context. States that he had an analytical mind and he put his ideas in a logical and systematic approach which put everything in a holistic context. Gives at the end American Library Association Resolution adopted by it on Jan 29, 1992.

GOPINATH, M A 35

Summary of the work and achievements of Dr S R Ranganathan, *Lib Sci Slant Docum & Inf Std* 29 (2) June 1992: 47-57.

Presents in this Summary the work and achievements of Dr S R Ranganathan in a chronological fashion. Arranges the contents under such headings as Summary of chief events, Endowments, Honours / Awards, Family, Education, Employment, Honorary work, Library Development Plans, Library Bills, Committee works in India and outside, Conferences in India and outside, Associations works, Library tours, Periodicals editing, Books published, Indian standards, Library catalogues, and Articles contributed.

GROLIER, ERIC de 36

Les politiques des bibliothesques, des services d 'information et l' heritage de Ranganathan (Library policies, information services and legacy of Ranganathan), *Bulletin d ' information de l' Association des Bibliothecaires Francais*, 158, 1993: 78-82.

Reports about the paper presented at the 58th IFLA General Conference held in New Delhi during 30 August-5 Sept 1992, surveying the career of Ranganathan in the context of current developments. Pays rich tributes to him on the occasion of his Birth Centenary Celebrations.

GROLIER, ERIC de 37

Library and information policy perspectives and Ranganathan's heritage, In *Papers*, 58th IFLA General Conference, New Delhi, 30 August - 5 Sept. 1992, pp 0.1 - 0.5.

Presented as the opening address in the Plenary Session of the 58th IFLA General Conference on 30th August 1992 at New Delhi. Discusses about Ranganathan's conceptual framework for national library and information policies, organization and design of national library systems, role of public, academic and special libraries in satisfying information needs, users and their needs, staff training and development, impact of national policies on scientific technological, cultural and social development, role of regional and international cooperation. Highlights the present value of Ranganathan's heritage.

HARJIT SINGH 38

S R Ranganathan - an exemplary teacher and a guide, *DESIDOC Bull* 12 (5) September 1992: 13-15.

Narrates author's experiences with Ranganathan and the profession of documentation while at Documentation Research and Training Centre, Bangalore as a student. Discovers qualities in Ranganathan as he made DRTC a *gurukul.* States that he was an interesting speaker with stories from *Puranas*, and equally prolific writer who believed in work only.

INDU BALA 39

Ranganathan- the reviver of library in India, *RMM*, 44-49.

Sheds light on the library in rags, housed in dingy corners of depleted buildings, chained and caged in cupboards and chests which, of course, had a glorious past. Describes how Ranganathan revived the spirit of the library by giving Five Laws, techniques of classification, initiating library movement and creating new dimensions in librarianship.

JAYARAJAN, P 40

Ranganathan's contributions- fundamental and seminal, *The Hindu* Sept 2, 1992.

Describes Ranganathan's works as seminal. States that Ranganathan's contributions to library science are significant, if not more, as those of Sir C.V.Raman to Physics and Ravindra Nath Tagore to literature.

JAYASWAL, P K 41

Ranganathan: A professional par excellence, *AGLIS JI* 9,1993 (Abstract only).

Traces the formulation of Five Laws based on Vedic philosophy, and correlates the sociological needs of the nation and their fulfillment through library service. Describes Ranganathan as a professional par excellence who had user and service at the forefront.

KATARIA, J K 42

Remembering Ranganathan, In *Souvenir* of CLA, 1992.

Praises Ranganathan while highlighting his qualities in the form of a poem. Describes him as ocean of knowledge, enforced laws of library science, gave us the reference service like Vivekanand's knowledge of God, his PMEST, etc helped in synthesis.

KAULA, P N 43

International Ranganathan Centenary Committee: Programme of activities, *Her Lib Sci* 31 (1-2) Jan - April 1992: 157-159.

States that the Committee is set up to celebrate the Birth Centenary of Dr. S R Ranganathan for which 70 papers from 26 countries have been collected to bring out a volume of papers. Explains about starting the Ranganathan Research Bulletin, collection of letters, postal stamp release, and showing a film on him, and special Centenary Number of library journals are being brought out in India and abroad as a mark of respect to the master.

KAULA, P N 44

Our indebtedness to Ranganathan, *RMM*, 1-15.

Delivered as a Keynote address on the occasions of the Punjab Library Association seminar organised as a part of Birth Centenary celebrations of Dr S R Ranganathan. Deals with the early life and career of Ranganathan, his entry into librarianship, creating of a new era in library and information science. Analyses Ranganathan's work and contributions. Identifies areas of work for study. Describes his impact on international librarianship, national and international recognition. Points out his simple, pious and dedicated life to the profession of librarianship which we must emulate.

KAULA, P N 45

Ranganathan remembered: Birth Centenary celebration, *Her Lib Sci* 32 (3-4) July - October 1993: 218 - 236.

Describes in brief the various events and celebrations of Ranganathan's Centenary beginning with Ranganathan International Centenary Committee constituted primarily by the author. Discusses international celebrations as IFLA 58th General Conference in New Delhi, ISKO Second Conference at Madras. Explains celebrations in India including seminars, lectures, book exhibitions, etc. Appends the ALA Resolutions on Ranganathan.

KAULA, P N 46

Remembering Ranganathan: His work in Delhi, *Her Lib Sci* 32 (1-2) Jan - April 1993: 54-69.

Mentions the invitations to Ranganathan for joining the University of Delhi, his appointment as Honorary Professor of Library Science in 1947, and his work in that capacity till 1955. Describes his work as the President of the Indian Library Association (1944-53) , work on projects and invitations from FID, UNESCO, IFLA, ISO, British Council. States Ranganathan's work in establishing Delhi Public Library, Indian National Scientific Documentation Centre, Union catalogue, Library Research Circles, professional journals, UGC Library Committee, UGC Review Committee. Refers to the Farewell Address on his departure from Delhi.

KAULA, P N 47

Remembering Ranganathan : His work in Delhi, *Jl of Lib & Inf Sci* 17(1) June 1992 : 17-32.

Describes the work carried out by S R Ranganathan from 1947 to 1955 during his stay as a Professor of Library Science at Delhi University. Discusses his activities as President of the Indian Library Association. Mentions about his tour of 1948 and participation in international activities. Enumerates his contribution to the development of libraries in India and research on library and information science. Concludes by referring to Ranganathan as "master educator".

KAULA, P N 48

S R Ranganathan as library scientist and benefactor, *In* G L Trehan and Girja Kumar : *Ranganathan Birth Centenary Monograph*, Chandigarh : Chandigarh Library Study Circle, 1993, p 36-d.

Describes Ranganathan as a library scientist par excellence, and the greatest benefactor. States that his contribution encompasses the entire domain of library and information science. Extracts taken from *Library Today* (Hyderabad) for Jan 1992.

KAULA, P N 49

Some episodes from Ranganathan's life, *Her Lib Sci* 32 (1 - 2) Jan - April 1993: 69-84.

Mentions the opportunity of the author to work closely with Ranganathan and plethora of correspondence between the two. Relates a number of episodes from the life and work of Ranganathan. States the episodes relating to his work: uncertainty in facet sequence, designing of classification, reference service, etc., relating to life : Single meal a day, no newspaper reading, no calling on highups, etc. and work as value of character, white bedsheet, faith in destiny, etc.

KAULA, P N 50

Works by and on Ranganathan published during the Centenary year: State of the art review, *Her Lib Sci* 32 (1-2) Jan -April 1993: 94-100.

Evaluates works published during the Birth Centenary year of Ranganathan which according to the author, includes 13 books, and 11 Special Numbers of journals published material on Ranganathan. Gives a review of all what is published during 1992.

KAULA, P N and VENKATAPPAIAH, V 51

Ranganathan International Centenary Volume Committee: An appeal, *IJILIS* 5 (1-2) Jan-June 1992: 153-156.

Makes an appeal about contributions for Ranganathan's Centenary Volume as he has been the master-architect in the domain of library science, library scientist par excellence, the great benefactor, world wide impact of his contribution, etc.

KHERA, RAJ 52

We owe our today to him, In *Souvenir* of CLA, 1992.

Regards Ranganathan as the Father of Library Science in India who brought overall development in the profession, and we owe everything to this great man who will always be worshipped by all seekers of informations. States that he by dint of hard work, attachment to a cause, worked for the welfare of the library staff in India.

KRISHAN KUMAR 53

Editorial, *Jl of Lib & Inf Sci* 17 (1) June 1992: 2 pages.

States in the Editorial of this Special Number of the *Journal of Library and information Science*, Volume 17, Number 1, June 1992 that it is brought out as a tribute to

Dr S R Ranganathan in the year of his Birth Centenary. Includes ten articles on and about the various aspects of the contribution of S R Ranganathan written by various scholars in the field including Prof P N Kaula, Girja Kumar, and others.

KRISHNA RAO , D B 54

Some facets of Ranganathan's personality, *In* G L Trehan and Girja Kumar : *Ranganathan Birth Centenary Monograph*, Chandigarh : Chandigarh Library Study Circle, 1992, pp 36.a - 36.c.

Reprinted from the *Herald of Library Science*, April-June 1973, describes Ranganathan as a store of Himalayan energy, had intense love for library science, was a symbol of work - chastity, and as a teacher used effective teaching methodology. Concludes that he was a great force in the library world for nearly fifty years who was respected in all countries of the world where library consciousness had developed.

KUMAR, P S G 55

Ranganathan ; a multi-faced personality, New Delhi : D K Publishers, 1992. xii, 240 p.

Tries to analyse the real librarian in Ranganathan, a master educator and a great humanist. Starts with a biographical note on him. Highlights Dr S R Ranganathan's outstanding contribution in various branches of librarianship in a systematic way and in a simple language. Studies the personality and philosophy of the man - Ranganathan and mysticism, a fitting tribute to Ranganathan in his Birth Centenary year as it gives a comprehensive view of Ranganathan and his work.

LANGRIDGE, D W

India and Ranganathan, *In* A J Meadow (Ed), *Knowledge and communication: Essays on the information chain*, London : Library Association, 1991, pp 13-15.

Discusses about the Indian librarian and library educator Dr S R Ranganathan and his contribution to the field of librarianship. Also points out its worldwide recognition and through him is the recognition of India, the country he was born in.

LANGRIDGE, D W 57

Ranganathan and mysticism, *SRR*, 26 - 27.

Explains the concept of 'Mysticism' the way Ranganathan used it, though he himself was not a mystic anyway. States that in his writings, the religious beliefs are implicit; through his continuous and wholeness approach to his works, he was termed as Karmayogi.

MANINDER YASH PAL SINGH 58

We owe our bread and butter to him, In *Souvenir* of CLA, 1992.

States that by enumerating Five Laws of Library Science, Ranganathan brought a revolution in libraries as books were made living things. Explains his manifold contributions to the field of library science. Describes him as the founder of the Indian Library Association and many other associations in different states. Mentions about his foreign tours, and his success in bringing libraries on par with teaching faculty. Pays gratitude and reverence to this great soul.

MARTIN, L M 59

Ranganathan for 90s : A conversation with Hemlatha Iyer (of the School of Information Science and Policy, SUNY Albany), *Technalities* 11, 1991: 12 - 14.

Reports about the conversation the author had with one of the Indian library science teacher settled in an American University. Describes about the relevance of Ranganathan's writings and contributions towards librarianship in the modern times when some changes are being effected as a result of the technological developments.

McILWAINE, I C 60

Ranganathan and University College, London, *RAW*, 32 - 41.

Describes in detail the association of Ranganathan since 1924 with the University College, London where he studied librarianship. Mentions about the papers he offered, record for which is still available in the College. Describes his experience, his remarks as the College student in London and that he is not forgotton there till today.

MITTRA, D K and KOTNALA, V 61

Dr S R Ranganathan : The path finder, *RAT*, 1-5.

Describes Ranganathan as a path finder to the library and information science as he engaged himself in finding 'path' for the betterment of the library profession. Gives in short early years of his life, his entry to the library field, his perception about the profession and his achievements in the field. Deals also with scene in India soon after Ranganathan's death. Gives his idea about "library service".

MOHANRAJAN, P A 62

Library science : Dr S R Ranganathan's contribution, 1924 -44, an analysis, Madras : Mohanvalli Publications, 1992. 112 p.

Brings together Ranganathan's earlier contribution as the First Librarian of the University of Madras. Discusses Ranganathan's experiments in organisation, administration, reference service, library classification, library cataloguing, and teaching of library science as a subject of study. Provides an insight into Ranganathan's working methodology. Includes a select list of his publications.

MOHANRAJAN, P A 63

The miracle man, *The Hindu*, August 9, 1992.

Gives a biographical sketch of Dr S R Ranganathan. Discusses his contribution to the field of librarianship, reflecting all facets of this miracle man in the world of library and information science who touched the height of it in and outside the country.

MOHANRAJAN, P A 64

S R Ranganathan, the miracle man, *In* G L Trehan and Girja Kumar : *Ranganathan Birth Centenary Monograph*, Chandigarh : Chandigarh Library Study Circle, 1993, pp 37-38.

Describes Ranganathan's achievements and contribution to the field of libraries and library science. Describes him as a miracle man who organised the Madras University Library so ably. Talks about his unfulfilled desire of a national enactment of public library law. Recounts the honours he got, the departments of library science he organised, the donations he gave to the University of Madras.

MOOKERJEE, SUBODH KUMAR 65

Sri Shiyali Ramamrita Ranganathan - a remeniscence, *College Lib* 8 (1-2) 1992 : 4 - 6.

Recollects meetings of the author with Dr S R Ranganathan from time to time. Discusses Ranganathan's unique contributions to the field of library and information science at the world level. Relates many interesting anecdotes and experiences of the meetings of the author with Dr Ranganathan.

MURTHY, S S 66

Editorial, *DESIDOC Bull* 12 (5) Sept 1992 : 2.

Speaks about the Special Issue of this Bulletin published by the Defence Scientific Documentation Centre, devoted to the memory of Dr S R Ranganathan, the father of the library movement in india, on the occasion of his Birth Centenary which falls on 12 August, 1992. Includes five articles on the life and work of Ranganathan in this Special Number.

NAGPAL, NEELAM 67

Had a will made of the hardest of steel, In *Souvenir* of CLA, 1992.

States that though born with poor health but his will was made of the hardest steel because of which he dominated the scene of Indian librarianship till his last day. Points out that he gave new dimensions to the library science by way of his contributions which were varied and many. States that he immortalised himself through his works and will continue to inspire generations to come.

NANAK, M P S G 68

Remembering Ranganathan today, *Information Management Report*, August 1992 : 12-14.

Outlines the career of Dr S R Ranganathan and his influence on library and information science theory. Describes briefly the influence of his Five Laws of Library Science and Colon Classification scheme.

NAVALANI, K and SATIJA, M P, *Eds* 69

Petits petals : A tribute to S R Ranganathan, New Delhi : ABC Publishing House, 1993. xiv (unnumbered), 150 p.

Includes 16 articles written by Indian and foreign contributors on life, works, personal experiences, and the effects of Ranganathan's ideas as felt in other countries. Describes more about Ranganathan's influence on classification, and on library practices in other countries, his efforts to institutionalise research in library science, etc. Pays tribute to Dr S R Ranganathan in his Centenary celebrations.

NAVALANI, K 70

The tallest torch bearer, *PP*, 117 - 122.

Explains about Ranganathan's interest in library movement and library legislation almost from the late 1920s. Describes about his efforts from 1933 which were largely unsuccessful, but he continued relentlessly to succeed in 1948. Discusses his passion for public library legislation and organised All India Seminar on Public Libraries in 1972 where he pleaded for National Grid of Public Library System for India.

NAVALANI, K and SATIJA, M P 71

Introduction, *PP*, ix - xiii.

Narrates the story of Ranganathan's life, education, entry in librarianship, training in United Kingdom, reorganisation of Madras University Library, writing of books on library and information science, coining new terminology, working at the Banaras Hindu University, Delhi University, Vikram University, Ujjain, establishing library associations, association with other bodies such as FID, etc, and the honours he received.

NEELAMEGHAN, A 72

Introduction, *Libri* 42 (3) July- Sept 1992: 171-175.

Writes about Ranganathan and his Danish connection in this Special Number of *Libri* (from Copenhagen), volume 42, Number 3, 1992 brought out as dedication to his work, and edited by the author. Includes eight papers on assessment of Ranganathan's contribution to classification, information retrieval, Five Laws of library science, his impact on international librarianship, etc and gives their resume.

PALMER, B I 73

Ranganathan as a person, *SRR*, 14-18.

Describes the life, education and contribution of Ranganathan to the field of librarianship. Trace his contact with Ranganathan and narrates some of the characteristic features of his personality.

PALMER, B I 74

Ranganathan, the man and his works: View through a bibliography (Biography Series 1), *Lib Sci slant Docum & Inf Std* 29 (2) June 1992: 99-108.

Reprinted from *Library Science slant to Documentation*, Vol 6 (3) September 1969: 273-288. Presents a review of the book *Essays in personal bibliography* (1967) compiled by A K Dasgupta on S R Ranganathan. Draws attention to the usefulness of the librametric study in bringing out the pattern of distribution of the works by and on Ranganathan by subjects, by quantity, by language, by period etc. Mentions briefly each of the major works of Ranganathan and its impact, commenting in particular the Five Laws, Colon Classification, Classified Catalogue Code, theory of library cataloguing, library development plans, and library legislation. Gives a glimpse of some aspects of Ranganathan's personality. Concludes with an appeal for updating the bibliography.

PANDURANGAM, S 75

Dr S R Ranganathan, 1892-1972 *ILS*, 3 p.

Recollects Ranganathan's association with the Institute of Library Science, Hyderabad, and he is remembered by many of its members. Describes his contribution to the field of library and information science and the importance he gave to small professional matters.

PARTHASARATHY, S 76

S R Ranganathan: made librarianship a profession, *The Hindu*, Madras, August 21, 1992.

Discusses about the life and contribution of Dr S R Ranganathan whose Birth Centenary year is being celebrated in 1992 by, among others, holding an international IFLA Conference in New Delhi. Describes Ranganathan as a man who made librarianship a profession.

PARTHASARATHY, S 77

Shiyali Ramamritam Ranganathan: Guest editorial, *Lib Sci slant Docum & Inf Std* 29 (2) June 1992: 43-45.

Highlights briefly in this Guest Editorial of this Special Number of the quarterly journal *Library Science with a slant to Documentation and Information Studies*, dedicated to the memory of Ranganathan, his work, contribution and achievements in the profession of librarianship who built libraries in Madras, Banaras Hindu University, Delhi, and also started teaching departments. Narrates his sojourn to Zurich, and then DRTC, Bangalore, his association with FID, IFLA, Classification Research Group (London), and other international bodies. Mentions that he had close association with spiritual persons also.

PUNJAB LIBRARY ASSOCIATION, PATIALA 78

Seminar on Ranganathan: Man and mission, held at Punjabi University, Patiala from April 29-30, 1994, Seminar papers, Patiala: Punjab Library Association, 1994. iv, 129 p.

Includes the Keynote address given by Prof P N Kaula on the occasion of the S R Ranganathan Centennial Seminar. Covers 14 articles written by authors from Punjab except one. Of these, two articles are in Punjabi. Four more papers were presented at the Seminar but those could not be included in the Seminar volume. The areas covered are many including Ranganathan's biographical note.

RAHA, SOMNATH 79

Dr S R Ranganathan: A profile, Calcutta: West Bengal College Libraries Association, 1992. 12p.

Provides a profile of Ranganathan pointing out the mission of his life to create and develop library movement in the country. Includes two papers - one in English and the other in Bengali presented at Dr S R Ranganathan Birth Centenary celebrations held on 9th August 1992 at Presidency College, Calcutta. Pays tribute to Ranganathan and discusses his life and mission.

RAJALAKSHMI, V AND PAL, R 80

Ranganathan and the Annals, *Ann Lib Sci & Docum* 39 (2) June 1992: 62-68.

Mentions that Ranganathan was the founder-editor of the *Annals* (1954-63). Analyses Ranganathan's contributions published in *Annals* (total 87, which is 50% of the total published in volume 1-10). Makes a subjectwise analysis revealing that 50% were on classification only. Reveals further that it was followed by cataloguing, documentation, teaching/training in library science, library and information science in general, standards, serials, and bibliographies. Gives a complete list of Ranganathan papers published in the *Annals*.

RANGANATHAN as a creative genius, library thinker 81

and humanist, *In* G L Trehan and Girja Kumar: *Ranganathan Birth Centenary Monograph*, Chandigarh: Chandigarh Library Study Circle, 1993, pp 14 c - 14.d.

Describes Ranganathan as a creative genius, thinker and humanist who gave his philosophy of librarianship in his Five Laws, and considered duty to do good to others. Describes Ranganathan as an intellectual giant, a scholar, a pattern maker, a protagonist of free book service for all.

RANGANATHAN as a creative writer, *In* G L Trehan 82

and Girja Kumar: *Ranganathan Birth Centenary Monograph*, Chandigarh: Chandigarh Library Study Circle, 1993, pp 15-18.

Describes Ranganathan as a creative writer who produced a corpus of library literature of about 60 books and a bumper crop of articles, research papers, speeches, addresses, messages, reviews, etc during the 50 years of his professional career. Discusses about his book Five Laws of Library Science. Explains impact of Ranganathan's writing as contained in Classified Catalogue Code and chain procedure. Describes the last phase of his life in which also despite failing health and blindness, he continued doing creative work. Mentions about his last wish also.

RANGANATHAN Birth Centenary: A watershed in librarianship (A Centenary report), *Lib Sci slant Docum & Inf Std* 29 (3) Sept 1992: 163-164. 83

Reports about the good response the Ranaganathan's Birth Centenary year recorded from several individuals and institutions in India and abroad including the 58th General IFLA Conference held at Delhi where Dr Grolier presented a review on Ranganathan; at Madras was held Second ISKO Conference; several books were published and special issues of several journals were also brought out in India and abroad. Mentions about the lectures delivered, stamp released, film produced, and so on.

RANGANATHAN in action at DRTC and writing work at home, *In* GL Trehan and Girja Kumar: *Ranganathan Birth Centenary Monograph*, Chandigarh: Chandigarh Library Study Circle, 1993, pp 19-23. 84

States that Ranaganathan was a Karmayogi who used

to work all the time at DRTC, Bangalore and at home also. Discusses about the ILA Conference at Bangalore in 1978, organised lectures under Sarada Ranganathan Endowment for Library Science, discussion of academic and professional problems, no coffee or tea to visitors, note book for communicating academic and professional matters, and his writing work at home on a charpoi, and thus continued doing research work.

RANGANATHAN International Centenary Volume Committee Invitation for contribution, *Her Lib Sci* 30 (3-4) July - Oct 1991: 239-240. 85

Reports an invitation to the professionals for contributions to be included in the Centenary Volume entitled 'International and Comparative Librarianship and Information Systems' to cover all aspects of library and information science of which Ranganathan was the fountain head during his life time.

REMEMBERING Ranganathan at Chandigarh, *In* G L Trehan and Girja Kumar: *Ranganathan Birth Centenary Monograph*, Chandigarh: Chandigarh Library Study Circle, 193, pp 43-44. 86

Discusses about the function organised by the Chandigarh Librarians Association and the T S Central State Library on November 26, 1992 to celebrate the Birth Centenary of Dr S R Ranganathan. Describes about the glowing tributes paid to Ranganathan in regard to his massive contributions to library profession, and who worked his entire life for the upliftment of the profession as for him it was only service to the society.

ROY, P B 87

Ranganathan; paying Gurudakshina, *Iaslic Bull* (3) Sept 1992: 137-143.

States that Ranganathan was not only a teacher but a Guru par excellence in library and information science.

Analyses some of his major contributions which help in solving current as well as future problems. Explains that the most appropriate *gurudakshina* would be to take steps in propagating and utilising Colon Classification and Classified Catalogue Code in all libraries and perpetuating them by producing manuals and workbooks in Indian languages, organising camp training courses, doing research, etc.

S R RANGANATHAN: A tribute, Calcutta: The National Library, 1993. 57 p. 88

Published as a tribute to Ranganathan in his Birth Centenary year by the staff members of the National Library (of India), Callcutta, it includes 11 papers, all by the library personnel of the National Library only, on the great Master's life, work and contributions. By publishing this monograph the National Library has acknowledged its debt to Ranganathan.

S R RANGANATHAN; A world 'librarian, 89

Library Times International 9 (1) July 1992: 14.

Written as Editorial, describes briefly the contribution of Ranganathan to libraries and librarianship in India, the books and articles he wrote, his library tours abroad, the awards he received, the honours he got, and the intonational seminars/conferences/meetings being held in the Birth Centenary year of the great man Ranganathan.

S R RANGANATHAN'S reminiscences of some 90

eminent personalities in the Punjab library world, *In* G L Trehan and Girja Kumar: *Ranganathan Birth Centenary Monograph*, Chandigarh: Chandigarh Library Study Circle, 1993, pp 39-42.

Describes S R Ranganathan's meetings with such library personalities of the state of Punjab as A C Woolner whom he met at the First Indian Library Conference in October 1933 in Calcutta, who has faith in the social value of libraries;

Lala Labhu Ram, librarian Punjab University, Lahore met Ranganathan at the same Conference; Rattan Chand Manchanda met him at Banaras in 1930 and at Madras in 1934; and Sant Ram Bhatia, Editor of the Modern Librarian and Indian Librarian. Ranganathan also met K M Asadullah from Punjab on various occasions, when he occupied the seat of dignity in the Imperial Library, Calcutta.

SARKAR, TAPAN 91

S R Ranganathan: A socialist leader of the century, *RAT*, 6-9.

Attempts to focus the socialist impact on Dr S R Ranganathan in reference to the socialist movement in the world. Turns to the definition and history of socialism. Presents Ranganathan in reference to the socialist movement of the 20th century who continued the legacy of the socialists, reassembeled the Fabian Socialists and devoted to the development of library and information science.

SATIJA, M P 92

Birth Centenary literature on Ranganathan: A review, *RMM*, 121 - 129.

Reviews the literature in the form of books and journals published on Dr S R Ranganathan during his Birth Centenary Year. Concludes that most of the literature is on classification, five laws, and their relevance in the information technology environment.

SATIJA, M P 93

Information sources on the life and work of Ranganathan, *Her Lib Sci* 32 (1-2) Jan - April 1993: 84-94.

Mentions the earliest bibliographies on Dr S R Ranganathan. Refers to the Ranganathan Festschrift, Volume 1 and 2. Mentions the British contribution, the doctoral work done on Ranganathan, special issues of journals brought out as memorial numbers on Ranganathan, his autobiography, and a number of works brought out in the Centenary Year.

SATIJA, M P 94

Life and mind of Ranganathan, *IJILIS* 5 (3-4) July - Dec 1992: 245-252.

Mentions about birth and education of S R Ranganathan. Explains the role of Ranganathan in librarianship in producing standard literature on librarianship. Discusses impact of Hindu Scriptures and some people on Dr S R Ranganathan.

SATIJA, M P 95

On his Birth Centenary, *DESIDOC Bull* 12(5) Sept 1992: 3-6.

Brings out a life sketch of S R Ranganathan as a legend. Gives account of the achievements and milestones he set during his life span and how the current status of libraries and profession differs from that of his dreams. Highlights the national and international recognition of his work, and the awards and laurels conferred to him.

SATIJA, M P 96

Padamshree S R Ranganathan - a legendary figure, a dreamer and a visionary, *In* G L Trehand and Girja Kumar: *Ranganathan Birth Centenary Monograph*, Chandigarh: Chandigarh Library Study Circle, 1993, p 36.

Outlines the most important events and achievements in Ranganathan's life. Showers praises on him for his immense contribution. Mentions about some of the awards and honour he received. States that he is being addressed the "Librarian to the World" by the American Library Association, and his time is also called as "Ranganathan Age".

SATIJA, M P 97

Ranganathan: Development of his writing career, *Lib Her* 29 (1-2) April-Sept 1990: 63-71.

Describes contribution of S R Ranganathan. Considers his Five Laws of Library Science as a fountainhead of his work. Regards Colon Classification as a second great breakthrough after Dewey. Points out that he recovered universal attention in his life time, his work won him wide acclaim. Concludes that he was having futuristic approach.

SATIJA, M P 98

S R Ranganathan and method of science, New Delhi: Aditya Prakashan, 1992. ix, 181 p.

Divided into 13 chapters revealing Ranganathan's insights, synthetic capacity, intution, etc. Discusses him as scientist who wanted to create research in library and information science. Describes the objective and systematic methods he followed in his writings. Developed from the author's Ph D work, it includes an appendix of Ranganathan's works.

SATIJA, M P 99

S R Ranganathan: The crusader, In *Souvenir*, Punjab Library Association, 1994, pp 1-4.

Gives an account of the birth, education, career, and functioning of S R Ranganathan at various places in India as Librarian and library and information science teacher. Mentions about his achievements, contribution to library and information profession at the global level.

SATIJA, M P 100

S R Ranganathan; a tribute, *Univ News* 30 (35) Aug 31, 1992: 151-153.

Describes birth, education, and librarianship of Ranganathan. Describes him as a prolific writer and author.

Discusses his contribution to facet analysis. Describes him as a crusador for Indian librarianship, yet he had international obligations and the world was a big family for Ranganathan who worked for international librarianship.

SATIJA, M P 101

S R Ranganathan: A tribute to the scientist, *LIS*, 168-172.

Describes life, works, and everlasting contributions to Indian librarianship by Dr S R Ranganathan. Discusses his role at international level and with such international agencies as Unesco, ISO, FID, etc.

SATYANARAYAN, R 102

Dr Ranganathan and library profession: A centenary, tribute, *Iaslic Bull* 37 (3) Sept 1992: 129-135.

States that the significance of Ranganathan's contribution to library and information service has not yet been assessed fully. Discusses in a general way his contribution of dynamic theory of classification, Colon Classification, symbiotic relationship between classification and subject indexing, formulation of POPSI, etc. Touches upon his association with FID, Unesco, his influence on PRECIS and AACR - 2, his role as a teacher and a crusader of library development and library legislation in India.

SEN, SUBIR K 103

Introduction, *Iaslic Bull* 37 (3) Sept 1992: 97-100.

Discusses about the materials published in this Special Number of the quarterly journal from Calcutta, *IASLIC Bulletin*, Volume 37 (3) September, 1992, brought out commemorating the Birth Centenary of Dr S R Ranganathan. Describes the potential area of research and study needed in respect of Ranganathan's personality and contributions. This special issue includes 11 articles by various Indian authors including three by Ranganathan himself. Also includes letters of Ranganathan with introduction by Gopinath. Mentions Ranganathan's links with IASLIC of which he was an honorary life member.

SETHI, A R 104

Aesthetics in Ranganathan, *Jl Lib & Inf Sci* 17 (1) June 1992: 89-101.

Points out that aesthetics and librarianship were quite close about 100 years ago but now they are not. Discusses concept of aesthetics. Examines aesthetics in Ranganathan's works, style and personality. Points out that Ranganathan termed his own intensive aesthethic experience as intuition and did not use the term "aesthetics" in his writings. Suggests that librarianship should come closer to aesthetics.

SHARIFY, NASSER 105

An encounter with a genius: A sentimental reflection on Ranganathan, *Her Lib Sci* 32 (1-2) Jan-Apr 1993 : 48-54.

Refers to the understanding of philosophy of S R Ranganathan. Describes first encounter with Ranganathan at the University of Pittsburgh, and the opportunity to act as his host. Narrates the first conversation with the genius of Ranganathan. Expresses gratitude for the personalised service to the great genius. Makes observation on his humility, his views on religion, his tackling of the entire field of library and information science. Refers to the honour of being awarded Kaula Gold Medal.

SHARIFY, NASSER 106

Remembering Ranganathan: A sentimental reflection, *RAW*, 149-157.

Describes author's interest in Ranganathan's works and contribution. Relates meeting with him at the Pittsburgh University, and their living together at author's residence, when Ranganathan narrated his life story. Discusses about the conversation that took place between the two professional personalities about the works and contribution of Ranganathan, about religion, intgegrity of knowledge, his mission to raise the status of Indian libraries and librarians etc.

SHARMA, N K 107

A tribute to Dr S R Ranganathan, *AGLIS JI* 9, 1993 (Abstract only).

Throws light on the different phases of S R Ranganathan's professional career and its impact on library and information science profession in India. Highlights his first contributions made to the field of librarianship which earned acclaim for him.

SHARMA, R N, *Ed* 108

S R Ranganathan and the West, New Delhi: Sterling Publishers, 1992. xvii, 179 p (Foreword by Patricia Glass Schuman, President ALA)

Published to celebrate the birth centenary of Dr S R Ranganathan, who introduced much needed reforms in Indian librarianship and made a deep impact on international librarianship. Includes 16 articles on the life and work of Ranganathan contributed by well known authors from Canada, USA and England. Brings out deep impact of Ranganathan on east west and therefore deserves to be recognised. Also includes a chronology of Ranganathan and the West. Gives also the two resolutions passed by the American Library Association during its mid-winter meeting held in January 1992 to celebrate Ranganathan's birth centenary.

SIDHU, A S 109

President speaks, In *Souvenir* of CLA, 1992. 2 p.

Tells that Dr S R Ranganathan was a tireless and dedicated scholar who emphasised the role of libraries in the society in continuing education, removal of illiteracy, agency for progress and development of a nation. States that the fittest tribute to Dr Ranganathan today would be to make every citizen of India library minded, as desired by him, and also to open the doors of our libraries to all those who long for these.

SRIVASTAVA, A P 110

Lasting impact of Ranganathan, *Ann Lib Sci & Docum* 39 (2) June 1992: 34-37.

Observes that Ranganathan strongly believed that knowledge represented real power. Discusses Ranganathan as a pattern maker in librarianship. Mentions how he welded ideas and practice of his age into coherent and convincing form of lasting value. Mentions about Ranganathan's Newtonian and Aristotelian approach of succinct analytical thinking. Describes him as one who had belief in God like Einstein and other great pattern makers. Explains the concept of pattern recognition which is needed to examine his work from a new angle. Mentions about modes of formation of knowledge. States that he was pioneer for computer scientists.

STILES, WILLIAM G 111

That's the way it is, *RAW*, 139-148.

Pays tribute to Ranganathan and states that he was a man ahead of his times. Mentions his contribution as a classificationist with a proper study of order. Relates experiences of meeting Ranganathan and learning many things from him, such as facet analysis and its use in reference work, his advice as to pass the examinations easily. Talks about Ranganathan and cognition, Personality perceived through what is left, and other fundamental categories, etc. Marks it a tribute from one librarian to another for his past efforts.

STRANGE but true, In *Souvenir* of CLA, 1992. 112

Puts forth some examples from the life of Ranganathan full of ups and downs, successes and defeats, bore the brunt and scars of many but left too much for us to emulate and follow his ideals. Mentions about his several strange likings, tastes which one would never believe, but are surely true.

SUBBA RAO, C V 113

Controversies on Dr S R Ranganathan, *PP* 13-20.

Narrates the stories about some of the controversies surrounding Ranganathan. Lists seven of such episodes from his professional life beginning from the University of Madras, and on other professional issues such as stock taking, salary scales, Colon Classification, etc.

SUKIASIAN, EDWARD 114

'Bud' iskrenen i chesten (be sincere and honest) *Par Biblioteka* No 7-8, 1992: 47-49.

Deals with life and work of the great Indian librarian and library educator, Dr S R Ranganathan, who has been sincere and honest throughout his life towards his profession of librarianship; and this was the advice he gave to the new generations of librarians. Pays tribute to Ranganathan in his birth centenary year.

SUTINDER SINGH 115

A moment of reflection: Editorial, *Univ News* 30 (35) Aug 31, 1992: 2.

Brought out as a Special Issue dedicated to the memory of Prof S R Ranganathan who is veritably described as the Father of Library Science in India. Deals with Ranganathan's life, career, achievements, contribution, honours and awards. Mentions about the holding of IFLA 58th General Conference in New Delhi in 1992 to honour Dr Ranganathan who had given his all to the cause of libraries and librarians.

TALWAR, B L 116

A consummate genius, In *Souvenir* of CLA, 1992.

Mentions Ranganathan as a onsummate genius in the field of library and information science in India who raised the status of the profession, fought for the service conditions of library personnel, and wanted the librarians to be dedicated and devoted to the cause of the profession. Salutes this great saint who sacrificed his life for the profession.

THAKUR, G S 117

A great genius, In *Souvenir* of CLA, 1992.

Showers praise on the great genius of library and information science Dr S R Ranganathan on the occasion of the bringing out an informative Souvenir on him during his Birth Centenary Year, 1992.

THUS SPAKE Ranganathan, In *Souvenir* of
CLA 1992. 118

Quotes from the great master his views on the profession, libraries, appeal to new generations of India, departmental libraries, research and university libraries, school and college libraries, library training, library facilities for research in LIS, development of library system according to a plan, avoid subscription library system, and value of library service and library legislation.

TREHAN, G L 119

A library prophet and a humanist, In *Souvenir* of CLA, 1992.

Lists briefly the major events of his life and major contribution of this library prophet, Ranganathan, to the library profession. Points out his Five Laws of Library Science revolutionised world's library thought.

TREHEN, G L 120

Looking back, at my contact with Ranganathan: lingering fragrance, *In* G L Trehan and Girja Kumar: *Ranganathan Birth Centenary Monograph*, Chandigarh: Chandigarh Library Study Circle, 1993 pp 7-14.

Discusses author's contacts with Dr. S.R Ranganathan. Deals with the study of Ranganathan's works, correspondence with him, and Ranganathan's remimiscences of Punjab library world, and so on.

TREHAN, G L and GRIJA KUMAR *et al* 121

Ranganathan Birth Centenary monograph: Padamshree S R Ranganathan- a creative genius and an intellectual par excellence, Chandigarh: Chandigarh Library Study Circle, 1993. 44 p.

Includes articles by such eminent Indian writers in librarianship as Girja Kumar, D B Krishna Rao, PN Kaula, P A Mohanrajan, G L Trehan, and others on the various facets of life and works of S R Ranganathan. Brought out on the occasion of Birth Centenary year of Padamshree S R Ranganathan by the Chandigarh Library Study Circle which celebrated the occasion on 26 November, 1992. It has a Foreword by K M Ujlambkar.

TREHAN, G L 122

Ranganathan Jayanti: S R Ranganathan a creative genius, *In* G L Trehan and Girja Kumar: *Ranganathan Birth Centenary Monograph*, Chandigarh: Chandigarh Library Study Circle, 1993, pp 1-5.

In this long poem, the author discusses about Ranganathan's life, birth, education, training abroad, career, professional contribution in the various fields. Makes special mention of his Five Laws of Library Science, facet analysis, Colon Classification, Prolegomena to library classification, fundamental categories, etc.

TREHAN G L 123

A tribute to Padamshree S R Ranganathan at his Birth Centenary 1992, *In* G L Trehan and Girja Kumar: *Ranganathan Birth Centenary Monograph*, Chandigarh: Chandigarh Library Study Circle, 1993, p 6.

Pays tribute to S R Ranganathan and his voluminous but scientific contribution to the field of library and information science, on the occasion of his Birth Centenary celebrations.

A TRENDSETTER, In *Souvenir* of CLA,1992 124

Explains the qualities of S R Ranganathan who worked for 18 hours a day and opened the library for maximum number of hours, and did unique work not for the sake of money but for serving his readers, and by dint of his hard work set many trends.

VERMA, I B 125

And we march on, In *Souvenir* of CLA,1992.

Discusses about the personality of S R Ranganathan, his contribution to the field of librarianship and library and information science education during the half a century he remained on the library scene. Mentions about the qualities of Ranganathan. Pays tribute to him on behalf of the Chandigarh Library Association.

WOOD, KATE 126

S R Ranganathan; a chronology, *SRR*, 28-35.

This chronology appended to the book produced by the Library Association, London (1973), republished in India for the first time in Ranganathan's Birth centenary year, 1992, is based on the earlier sources such as Ranganathan Festschrift Volume 1, Essay in personal Bibliography, Festschrift Volume 2, and other sources, and hence is not up-to-date.

YAHYA HAROON,K 127

An epic portrayed, *Her Lib Sci* 31 (1 - 2) Jan- Apr 1992: 83-87.

Reviews the autobiographical work of S R Ranganathan, *A Librarian looks back* which is divided into three parts. Part A includes chapters on professional career of Ranganathan. Part B is devoted to his professional contribution through associations, library legislation, etc. Part C deals with Ranganathan's personal glimpses at various phases of his life and work, contribution, honours and awards, chronology of life and list of major publications by and on him.

COMPARATIVE BIOGRAPHY

GIRJA KUMAR 128

Ranganathan, Dewey and C V Raman : A study in the arrogance of intellectual power, New delhi : Har Anand Publications, 1991. 147 p.

Divided into six chapters and an interesting Supplement "Ranganathan as the historical being". Makes a comparative biography of the three great men Raman - a great physicist and Noble Laureate, and Ranganathan and Dewey - the greats of library science. Describes them in terms of accumulating, assimilating and retaining power for purpose of intellectual pursuit, and ego satisfaction. Traces their life histories, achievements, etc; similarities and dissimilarities in the three characters. Points out the week points of the three great men.

KUMAR, P S G 129

Kaula and Ranganathan : A perspective, *In* V Ventatappaiah (Ed), *Dimensions in library and information science*, New Delhi : Concept Publishing Company, 1991, pp 523 - 533.

Presents an analysis of the work of P N Kaula and

that of S R Ranganathan pointing out latter's impact on Kaula as librarian, teacher, Editor, project designer. Refers to the work that Kaula did for S R Ranganathan in popularising his ideas. Also records views of S R Ranganathan on P N Kaula.

VENKATAPPAIAH, V 130

Iyyanki, Ranganathan and Kaula, *Her Lib Sci* 30 (1 - 2) Jan - Apr 1991 : 3-8.

Mentions pioneering work of S R Ranganathan, I V Ramanayya and P N Kaula. Describes the work of Iyyanki and his contact with S R Ranganathan. Refers to the observations of Ranganathan about Andhra Pradesh library movement causing adverse reaction from I V Ramanayya, and subsequent withdrawl of the statement by Ranganathan. States also the observations of I V Ramanayya on the work of P N Kaula and his association with library movement in Andhra Pradesh.

LETTERS OF RANGANATHAN

LETTERS OF Ranganathan - I, *Iaslic Bull* 37 (3) Sept 1992 : 187-202. 131

Includes six letters from Bernard Palmer / Ranganathan correspondence collection covering the period from 1949 to Ranganathan's death. Gives an insight into Ranganathan's personality and developments of his thoughts on classification. These letters are published in this Special Number of *Iaslic Bulletin* courtesy of Mr. Russel Bowden of Library Association (UK), and Mr. S C Biswas, New Delhi. The collection is presently housed in the Information and Library Studies Library at the University College of Wales, Aberystwyth.

LETTERS OF Ranganathan - II, *Iaslic Bull* 37 (3) Sept 1992 : 203-217 132

Presents the text of 13 letters between Ranganathan and Mahalanobis, with an introduction by M A Gopinath (of

D R T C). Indicates not only warmth and friendship but also abiding interest they had in the development of the Documentation Research and Training Centre, as a centre for research, development, education in library, and documentation and information science.

LETTERS OF Ranganathan - III, *Iaslic Bull* 37 (3) Sept 1992 : 219-229. 133

Includes 13 letters written to different persons on different occasions at different times, and on different subjects. The letters reveal Ranganathan's deep concern and involvement with the issues and problems of the profession as well as the careers of the students and young librarians. The letters were addressed to B Guha, B K Ghosh, Amitabha Chatterjee, among others.

AWARDS AND HONOURS

AWARDS & HONOURS, In *Souvenir* of CLA, 1992. 134

Mentions some of the awards and honours Ranganathan received both at home and abroad. States that he was the first and the only librarian so far to get so many awards and honours including honorary D Litt by the University of Pittsburgh, and the University of Delhi, title of Rao Sahib, and Padamshri by the Government of India, National Research Professor in Library Science, and so on.

CONFERENCES

IFLA CONFERENCE ON RANGANATHAN

CHATTERJEE, AMITABHA 135

World comes to India : A momentous meet of librarians, *Iaslic Bull* 37 (4) Dec 1992 : 277 - 290.

Traces the background of holding of the 58th General Conference of IFLA in Delhi in 1992. Gives a summarised description of various events such as pre-Conference seminar,

COMLA Workship, Indo- US- SAARC Conference of library and information science profesionals, satellite meetings, inaugural session, celebration of birth centenary of S R Ranganathan, various lectures, various bodies meetings, technical sessions, the exhibition, the IFLA Express, the special issues and publications, the visits, resolutions taken. Gives a short resume of interview with the President and Secretary- designate of IFLA.

FREEMAN, M 136

Indian days : Recollection of IFLA 1992 New Delhi and Ranganathan Centenary roadshow, *Focus on Int & Comparative Librarianship* 23 (3) Dec 1992 : 107 - 109.

Reports about the U K contribution to 58th IFLA Conference held in New Delhi during 30 August - 5 September, 1992. Covers also Ranganathan Centenary lecture tour of India focussing on the contribution made by the United Kingdom.

GOPINATH, M A 137

58th IFLA General Conference (30th August - 5 September 1992, New Delhi) on library and information policy perspectives, *Lib Sci slant Docum & Inf Std* 29 (4) Dec 1992 : 213-216.

Reports in detail about the Inauguration of the 58th General IFLA Conference held in New Delhi on the occasion of Dr S R Ranganathan's Birth Centenary Year. Discusses about the Plenary Session with Dr Eric de Grolier as the speaker. Reports on Sectional meetings on Mobile libraries, Bibliographical control, Classification and indexing, Editors of library journals, Parliament libraries, Interlending and Document delivery, Acquisition and Exchange, Library theory and Research, National Libraries, etc.

IFLA : CONFERENCE theme and programme (30 Aug-5 Sept, 1992) *NISSAT Newsletter* 11 (2) Apr-June 1992: 10-11. 138

Mentions the three main themes of the 58th General Conference of IFLA to be held during the 30 Aug-5 Sept, 1992 at New Delhi. States that the Plenary Session will be addresses by Eric de Grolierr with the main focus on Dr S R Ranganathan.

IFLA 58TH GENERAL Conference, New Delhi: An international festival for librarians in India, *NISSAT Newsletter* 11 (4) Oct-Dec 1992 : 3 - 11. 139

Describes the event held in New Delhi during 30 Aug - 5 Sept 1992, attended by 1324 delegates and organised by the Indian Library Association. Discusses the Inauguration by Human Resource Development Minister Arjun Singh, and speeches by IFLA President, and others. States that the Plenary Session was addressed by Dr Eric de Grolier who spoke on the relevance of Dr Ranganathan. Mentions about other special features of the IFLA Conference.

KALIA, D R 140

IFLA General Conference 1992, New Delhi, *CLIS Observer* 9(3-4) July-Dec 1992 : 47-56.

Gives report about the 58th General Conference of IFLA held in New Delhi from 30 August to 5 September 1991. States that in all 832 participants came from abroad, and 358 from India. Mentions that in all 137 papers were submitted of which 80 were printed and circulated. Gives a country wise break of the participants in Appendix - I. Gives a list of papers presented at the Conference.

KAULA, P N 141

The opportunity of a century : Time for introspection, *Her Lib Sci* 31 (3-4) July-Oct 1992: 250-252.

Discusses the appeal made by the author in the Birth Centenary Year of Dr S R Ranganathan , when 58th IFLA Conference was held in New Delhi during 30 Aug - 5 Sept 1992 sponsored by the Indian Library Association. Appeals that the income that ILA has made out of this international Conference should be properly used such as in setting up of an Endowment and Research institution in Commemoration of Ranganathan.

INTROSPECT and prospect : Conference participation, *NISSAT Newsletter* 11 (4) Oct-Dec 1992: 20-24. 142

Explains about the participation of 1294 delegates from 80 countries, with 410 participants from India, at the 58th IFLA General Conference held at New Delhi to commemorate the Birth Centenary of Dr S R Ranganathan. Discusses about the technical content as IFLA - 92 was preceded by ten seminars / workshops and followed by one.

KRISHAN KUMAR 143

A momentous library conference, *The Hindu*, Delhi, Sunday, Aug 30, 1992, Special Feature, A.

Describes about the 58th General Conference of IFLA being held in New Delhi from Aug 30 to Sept 5, 1992 to coincide with the Birth Centenary celebrations of Dr S R Ranganathan in which about 1500 delegates are likely to participate. States that there will be exchange of information with librarians from all over the world, holding of book exhibitions, literary project, etc. Calls it the biggest conference to be held in the history of Indian librarianship.

LAHIRI, A 144

The jamboree that was, *NISSAT Newsletter* 11 (4) Oct-Dec 1992: 1.

Discusses about the IFLA - 92 held in New Delhi, the biggest event of the century for the librarians and information scientists in India, which was organised here to mark the Birth Centenary Year of the great Indian librarian Dr S R Ranganathan.

MANGLA, P B and SATIJA, M P 145

IFLA General Conference, New Delhi, 1992, *Int Lib Move* 15 (1) Mar 1993: I-V.

Reports about the 58th IFLA General Conference held in New Delhi in commemoration with Dr S R Ranganathan's Birth Centenary year, during 30 Aug - 5 Sept 1992. Reports about the inauguration, the key theme, important issues discussed and resolutions passed, etc.

NATIONAL Policy on libraries in offing, *The Hindu*, 31st August 1992. 146

Reports about the inauguration of the 58th IFLA General Conference held in New Delhi on 30th August 1992 by the Human Resource Development Minister, Arjun Singh who said that the policy of library and information system will be implemented in the next five years.

RANGANATHAN Birth Centenary: A watershed in librarianship (A centenary report), *Lib Sci Slant Docum & Inf Std* 29 (3) Sept 1992: 163-164. 147

Presents a report about Ranganathan's Birth Centenary year which recorded a good response from several individuals and institutions from India and abroad such as IFLA Conference held in New Delhi at the invitation of the Indian Library Association. In the Plenary Session, Dr Eric de Grolier, a contemporary of Dr Ranganathan since Dorking Conference days, presented a review on Ranganathan. Gives also account of other conferences also held in commemoration of Ranganathan's birth centenary year. These include Third International Conference on Informetics (Bangalore, 1991), DRTC Workshop, etc. Makes a mention of the special publications, Special Numbers of several periodicals dedicated to the memory of Ranganathan, lectures, postal stamp etc.

RANGRA, V K 148

IFLA-92 and the Third World, *Patriot*, Sept 28, 1992.

Describes the IFLA-92 Conference held in Delhi to mark the Birth Centenary of Dr S R Ranganathan as a club of Western Librarians to a large extent. Feels that the cause of the Third World Librarians was neglected, though IFLA has a special section on Advancement of Librarianship in the Third World (ALP).

THE RESOLUTIONS, *NISSAT Newsletter* 11 (4) Oct-Dec 1992: 29-32. 149

Gives resolutions adopted at the IFLA 58th General Conference, 1992 on the topics of discussion such as Government support, socio-cultural impact, Education and training, professional associations, standards and guidelines, user satisfaction, case studies, etc.

RESOLUTIONS passed at the IFLA Conference held at New Delhi from August 30 to September 5, 1992, *CLIS Observer* 10 (1-2) Jan-June 1993: 37-40. 150

Lists various Resolutions topic by topic, passed at the 58th General Conference of IFLA held at New Delhi to celebrate the birth centenary of Dr S R Ranganathan the great Indian Liabrarian who got world wide acclaim.

SECOND ISKO CONFERENCE ON RANGANATHAN

ASUNDI, A Y, SRIDHAR, APARNA and SREELATHA, G 151

Second International ISKO Conference on Cognitive Paradigms in Knowledge Organisation: A review, *Lib Sci slant Docum & Inf Std* 29 (4) Dec 1992: 217-222.

Reports in detail about the Second ISKO Conference held at Madras during 26-28 August organised as part of Ranganathan Centenary celebrations. Reports about the inauguration and the eight Technical Sessions in which 29 papers were presented by authors from 15 countries.

DAHLBERG, I 152

Second International ISKO Conference, Madras, Aug 26-28, 1992, *Int Classif* 19 (1) 1992: 159-161.

Reports about the Second International Conference organised by ISKO with Madras Library Association in which some 70 participants from 12 countries participated. The papers presented at the Conference were published in book form. Gives a detailed report about the Conference with photograph.

CHANDIGARH LIBRARIANS ASSOCIATION CONFERNENCE ON RANGANATHAN

CENTENARY celebration, 1992 ; a report, In *Souvenir* of CLA, 1992.

Reports about the programmes and activities of Chandigarh Librarians Association which organised functions throughout the year of 1992 to celebrate the Birth Centenary of Dr S R Ranganathan. It organised such activities as Slogan writing contest, Cartoon making contest, Essay writing, Exhibition of charts, Ranganathan stamp release function, etc.

MADRAS LIBRARY ASSOCIATION

MALA 154

Report of the Executive Committee, 1 April 1992-31 March 1993, Madras : MALA, 1993.

Presented at the 50th meeting held in Madras on 19 June 1993. Contains a detailed report of the various activities of MALA as well as others associated with the celebrations of the Birth Centenary of Dr S R Ranganathan. Gives also information about the publications in tthe form of books and journals brought on the occasion.

RANGANATHAN AND PROFESSIONAL ASSOCIATIONS
RANGANATHAN AND IASLIC

MUKHERJEE, NIRMALENDU 155

Dr Ranganathan and the Iaslic, *Iaslic Bull* 37 (3) Sept 1992 : 155-161.

Gives as account of the views Dr S R Ranganathan expressed about the Indian Association of Special Libraries and Information Centres (Calcutta). Analyses these views and shows how far these are justified and relevant in the present context. Also observes that many of these ideas of Ranganathan were taken up by the IASLIC in later years.

RANGANATHAN AND ILA

KUMAR, P S G 156

Ranganathan and Indian Library Association, In *Souvenir* of 39th All India Library Conference, Department of Public Libraries, Government of Karnataka, Bangalore, 7-10 January 1994, pp 71-73.

Mentions Ranganathan's association with ILA since its inception. Describes his contribution in finalising the ILA constitution and intellectual contribution at the conferences. Discusses Ranganathan's contribution as President of ILA by redrafting the constitution, organising conference regularly, accelerating the publication programme, compiling a *Directory of Indian libraries* undertaking Union catalogue project, starting of *Abgila* etc.

IMPACT OF RANGANATHAN ON INTERNATIONAL / WORLD LIBRARIANSHIP

COBLANS, H 157

Ranganathan in the international scene, *SRR*, 22-25.

Comments on the international impact of Dr S R Ranganathan and his contribution right from the day of his honorary membership of the FID in 1957. Discusses about his being invited by UNESCO, his association with the Classification Research Group (London), International Organisation of Standards, IFLA meetings, the honour and awards he received including the D Litt degree from the University of Pittsburgh. Concludes by saying that he became a "conscience" for the West - a corrective for their assumptions on name forms, cataloguing rules, classification prejudices, etc.

FOSKETT, D J 158

Ranganathan's impact on world librarianship, *In* Naimuddin Quereshi and Zahiruddin Khurshid (Eds), *Trends in international librarianship*: A festschrift honouring Anis Khurshid, Karachi: Royal Book Company, 1991.

Discusses about the contribution made and role played by the great Indian library scientist that his impact has been realised at the world librarianship. Describes Ranganathan's association with many international bodies such as FID, IFLA, Unesco, ISO, for which he went on lecture tours, the Classification Research Group (London) which followed his classificatory principles, the honours and awards he got abroad, and so on.

KABIR, A F M FAZLE 159

Ranganathan: The educator and his influence on the Western world, *RAW*, 61-70.

Relates the contribution Dr S R Ranganathan made to the library education in India through discussion-based teaching, and was equally well known for his teaching excellence in the West. Also discusses his influence on library practice, classification, service philosophies. Concludes that Ranganathan was a "Renaissance Man" and it certainly seems the "Age of Ranganathan" which will continue to be with the library world for years to come and continue to provide a base for the realisation of the concept of total library service.

KAULA, P N 160

Impact of Ranganathan's concepts and techniques on international librarianship, *Her Lib Sci* 32 (1-2) Jan-April 1993: 36-43.

Refers to the two phases in the world librarianship: Pre-Ranganathan era and Ranganathan -era. Describes the beginning of Ranganathan era with the publication of Five Laws of Library Science. Mentions international contacts and advisory role of Ranganathan with such agencies as the United Nations, FID, UNESCO, ISO, IFLA. Evaluates the work of Ranganathan at international level, the honours and awards given to him. Mentions high tributes paid by distinguished personalities and associations including the Library Association (UK), and Amercian Library Association.

RANGANATHAN and the West: A Chronology, *RAW*, 174-177. 161

Outlines the events, arranged in chronological order, in the life and career of Dr *S R Ranganathan* beginning from his birth on 12 August, 1892 to his death on 27 September, 1972. Mentions only those dates which concern his visits to the Western countries. It is reprinted from S R Ranganathan 1892-1972, edited by Edward Dudley, London: The Library Association, 1974, pp 33-40, and also from *Library Science Today*: Ranganathan Festschrift, Volume I, edited by P N Kaula, Bombay: Asia Publishing House, 1965, pp 779-782.

SHARMA, RAVINDRA N 162

Ranganathan and the West, *RAW* 158-169.

Discusses the contribution made by Ranganathan to librarianship. Describes his impact on the West and the honour he received from various institutions. Gives the importance of his Five Laws of Library Science for which the West has been grateful to him. Narrates his travels from East to West because of his involvement of in the Western and international librarianship. Discusses Colon Classification and the Classified Catalogue Code, and their impact on Western librarians. Mentions about his lectures trips to the West. Explains his contribution to terminology for introducing many new words to the field of library and information science. Mentions about the tributes paid to him after his death. Concludes that Ranganathan was the leader of the profession, and the unquestioned giant of 20th century library science.

SHARMA, RAVINDRA N 163

Ranganathan's impact on international librarianship through information technology, *Libri* 42 (3) July-Sept 1992: 258-267.

Describes briefly, with extensive review, the impact of Ranganathan's contributions to international librarianship, especially in Europe and the USA. States that application of information technology (IT) in library and information science has not diminished the value of his contributions; and rather more areas of their usefulness are being identified. Also that IT is enabling the realisation of Ranganathan's vision of a user-centered, user-friendly information service implied in his Five Laws of Library Science.

RANGANATHAN AND DENMARK

FRIIS-HANSEN, JENS, B and ENGEL, SVEND 164

Impact of the contributions of Ranganathan in Denmark, *Her Lib Sci* 32 (1-2) Jan-Apr 1993 : 44-47.

Mentions the study of work of S R Ranganathan by Danish librarians. Describes the influence of Ranganathan on various writings in Denmark, particularly of Kirkegaard, Jenson, Hansen, etc. Reproduces excerpts from the Kaula Endowment Lecture delivered by Kirkegaard, tribute paid to Ranganathan and the homage paid by Hansen on passing away of Ranganathan. States that theories propounded by Ranganathan are studied at Danish Royal School of

Librarianship. Mentions about his visit to Copenhagen to deliver lectures. Illustrates the influence of Dr Ranganathan on Danish librarianship.

RANGANATHAN AND RUSSIA

SUKIASIAN, EDWARD R 165

The ideas of Ranganathan in Russia : Results and tendencies, *Int Classif* 19 (1) 1992 : 7-9.

Presents a short survey of studies made in Russia during the past 45 years concerning the work of S R Ranganathan, especially with regard to his classification terminology, the chain procedure and the categorical analysis for the application in the alphabetic subject index and the classified catalogue. Also shows how the knowledge of facetization was used for the improvement of UDC and LBC. Points out work done in information retrieval on the basis of Ranganathan's ideas.

SUKIASIAN, EDWARD R 166

Ranganathan i Sovetskoe bibliotekovedenie (S R Ranganathan and Soviet library science), *Soviet Bibl* No.1, 1992: 87-102.

Discusses about the contribution of Ranganathan that have influenced the librarians and library science in the erstwhile Soviet Union (now Russia). Points out about the admiration the Russian librarians have developed for Dr Ranganathan in recognition of his contribution and the seminal thoughts he put forward to improve the library services.

SUKIASIAN, EDWARD R 167

Ranganathan and the Soviet Union, *Lib Sci slant Docum & Inf Std* 29 (2) June 1992: 65-76.

Identifies the various features that have led to a culture-bond between India and Soviet Union. Presents the various events that have led to the admiration of Dr S R Ranganathan commends in the Soviet Union. Analyses the contribution of Ranganathan and recommends greater attention towards the seminal contributions to library science and service.

RANGANATHAN AND UK

HARRISON, K C 168

Ranganathan and British librarianship, *RAW* 17-31.

Mentions briefly S R Ranganathan's early years. Describes the first visit of Ranganathan to England in 1924 to study librarianship, and his interest in classification led to the publication of Colon Classification in 1933. Brings out relationship between Ranganathan and B I Palmer, and Five Laws, Colon Classification and chain indexing began to be studied in England. Discusses impact of Ranganathan on British National Bibliography through his classificatory principles; and his faceted ideas were discussed. Brings out relationship of Ranganathan with Maurice Gwyer in Delhi; Ranganathan's library tour of England in 1948, meeting British librarians, his contribution to *The Library World*, a British monthly journal. Mentions about the British tribute paid to him at his death in 1972.

HUNTER, ERIC J 169

Ranganathan UK: The influence of Ranganathan's work on the development of classification and indexing in the United Kingdom, *PP*, 77-91.

Narrates importance of faceted classification in computer which finds its origin to Ranganathan. States that Ranganathan's theories went to West because of Berned I Palmer (a close friend of Ranganathan), and then A J Wells through chain indexing in British National Bibliography. Describes role of Classification Research Group in spreading Ranganathan's classificatory ideas, and production of special classification schemes based on faceted principles, the thesaurofacets, Bibliographic Classification-2. Broad System of Ordering, etc.

RANGANATHAN AND USA

COCHRAINE (ATHERTON), PAULINE 170

The influence of Ranganathan upon library and information science, library education, and me, *RAW*, 50-60.

Describes the significance and depth of the Five Laws of Library Science propounded by Dr S R Ranganathan as they offer guidance and rationale we (the Americans) need. Discusses the influence of Law 2 on need for use studies, improving catalogue use, focus on the reader, principle of least action, and cooperation. Discusses influence of Law 3 on catalogue and readers' requirements, with regard to the structure of catalogue. Discusses influence of Law 5 on the human side, professional education, the challenge of change in library education, change of attitude, relating library education to library problems. Acknowledges Ranganathan's influence on her philosophy of library science. Outlines a chronology of Ranganathan- (Atherton) Cochrane relationship.

COMAROMI, JOHN P 171

Ranganathan's influence on American librarianship, *PP* 123-129.

Explains how Dr S R Ranganathan's ideas entered the United States of Amercia via United Kingdom where they did not stir much initially, and had no immediate effect on library classification. States that Ranganathan provided a rationale and a vocabulary for classification construction such as facet analysis. Describes about the influence of Ranganathan on Dewey Decimal Classification, the latest editions.

COMAROMI, JOHN P 172

Ranganathan's influence on American librarianship, *RAW* 10-16.

Traces the beginning of Ranganathan's relationship with America to his dialogue with Henry E Bliss, and subsequent comparison of Colon Classification and the Bibliographic Classification. Discusses the influence of Ranganathan's Five Laws of Library Science upon the practice of American librarianship. States that Ranganathan provided a rationale and a vocabulary for classification construction, facet analysis. Discusses the roots of PRECIS in Ranganathan's classificatory ideas, his substantial influence on Dewey Decimal Classification and its revisions. Concludes that but for Ranganathan's ideas the Americans may not have at their disposal the analytical tools that Melvil Dewey did not provide them.

FINKS, LEE W and HAUG, JAMES D 173

Ranganathan's contribution to American librarianship, *RAW*, 71-97.

Pays personal tributes (by the first author) to Dr S R Ranganathan. Attempts to measure Ranganathan's influence in a quantitative manner by using the methods of a combination of citation and content analysis to the entire population of articles in American and Canadian publications which refer to or review Ranganathan's articles and books cited in *Social Science Citation Index*, and *Library Literature*. Concludes that Ranganathan's publications had influence upon Amercian and Canadian authors particularly in the subject of classification, and they also recommended his works favourably.

KONNUR, M B 174

Dr S R Ranganathan and American librarianship: *In* V Venkatappaish (Ed), *Dimensions of library and information science: Kaula festschrift:* Papers contributed in honour of Prof P N Kaula on his sixtyfirst birth day, New Delhi: Concept Publishing Company, 1991, PP 297-301.

Narrates the impact of the works and contribution of Dr S R Ranganathan on American librarianship. Refers to the tributes paid to the importance of the work of Ranganathan that he has been called as 'World Librarian'.

KONNUR, M B 175

Dr S R Ranganathan: American view, *PP*, 131-137.

Explains about Dr S R Ranganathan's ideas propounded through his writings on classification and cataloguing in particular, in American thinking in these fields. Discusses also Ranganathan's concept of pre-natal classification and cataloguing, his Five Laws of Library Science. Mentions about Ranganathan and the American honours bestowed upon him in recognition of the importance of his works.

SHARMA, RAVINDRA N 176

Ranganathan and the United States, *PP*, 136-146.

States that Ranganathan was the only librarian to have contributed to all branches of library and information science which made him famous. Writes about his contributions to classification, cataloguing, the honours he was given, the terminology he introduced, tributes and views displaying the American influence.

RANGANATHAN'S CONTRIBUTIONS TO LIBRARIANSHIP/LIBRARY AND INFORMATION SCIENCE

ANNAMALAI UNIVERSITY, DEPARTMENT OF LIBRARY AND INFORMATION SCIENCE, ANNAMALAI NAGAR 177

Dynamics of librarianship; felicitation to luminaries in the profession - Birth Centenary publication of Dr S R Ranganathan, Annamalai Nagar: Department of Library and Information Science, Annamalai University, 1992. x, 327+14 (unnumbered) p.

Includes 32 articles divided into four Sections. Section A- Memorabilia (5 Papers): Section B- Papers on Ranganathan's contribution (Papers 6-12); Section C - Library and Information Science Education (Papers 13-22) Section D-Other areas (Papers 23-32). This publication is brought out as Birth Centenary Publication of Dr S R Ranganathan, and as a felicitation to luminaries in the profession such as V Durairajan and S R Ranganathan.

BARUA, P 178

Ranganathan's contribution to library science: A brief appraisal, *College Lib* 8 (1-2) 1992: 7-10.

Mentions that there are greatmen in every walk of life and Dr S R Ranganathan was one of them in Library Science. Gives his birth and education. Explains his role as a teacher and librarian at the University of Madras, Banaras Hindu University, and University of Delhi. Discusses the honours and fellowships Ranganathan received. Describes his contribution to the subjects of classification, cataloguing and indexing, library movement, etc.

BHATTACHARYYA, G 179

Ranganathan: An outstanding philosopher of science, *Lib Sci slant Docum & Inf Std* 29 (2) June 1992: 59-64.

Presents an analysis and approach to scientific method and the criteria for deeming a subject-field as a science. Analyses contributions to this modelling. Identifies Ranganathan's spiral of scientific method as a basic model to the field which is an elegant approach as that of Thomas Kuhn. Feels that this contribution of Ranganthan is a seminal one.

BORAH, BHADRA and GOSWAMEE, BHUPEN, *Eds* 180

Librarianship in North-east India: A souvenir to comm - emorate the Silver Jubilee Celebration, Department of Library and Information Science, Gauhati University, 4-5 July 1992, Guwahati: Department of Library and Information Science, Gauhati University, 1992. xvi, 146 p.

Includes 12 articles in English and eight articles in Assamese on different aspects of library and information science in this Souvenir brought out on the occasion of the Silver Jubilee of the Department of LIS, Gauhati University. It is fondly dedicated to the late Dr S R Ranganathan, Father of Library Science in India and late Dr R L Mittal.

FOSKETT, D J 181

Ranganathan's professionalism, *SRR*, 19-21.

Remembers Dr S R Ranganathan as a 'Whole man' who, in his writings, interpreted his approach to the profession of librarianship. Describes his guiding principles by which one should act, and these embody in his Five Laws of Library Science. States that Ranganathan was an internationalist by his approach, and he always acknowledged his debts to Dewey.

GOPINATH, M A 182

Ranganathan's concept of "live library" and the role of the library profession, *DL*, 14-28.

Describes Ranganathan's achievements in library profession. Discusses his Five Laws of Library Science and his views on emerging library service, and the new emerging dimensions of the profession. Describes impact of information systems development, information resource management. Narrates information science and its connection with other disciplines. Gives purposes of library as given by Dr Ranganathan and mentions about his integral approach.

GUPTA, A K 183

Ranganathan and the library science, *College Lib* 8 (1-2) 1992: 11-13.

Mentions about the birth and death of Ranganathan, and his reluctance to embrace librarianship. Discusses his contribution with reference to the totality of librarianship, as he himself was a complete man, dedicated to his profession. Observes that Ranganathan's activity level throughout his life time reflects a total, selfless commitment to library science.

GUPTA, S R 184

Institute of Chartered librarian: A conceptual framework, *Jl Lib & Inf Sci* 17 (2) Dec 1992: 143-157.

Justifies the need for professional consultancy for libraries on the basis of observations and findings of a research study of college libraries in India. Distinguishes between instrument of certification and instrument of licensing in a profession. Points out that so far only certification is being done by library and information science schools. Argues that licensing is required to prepare library consultants who may be called as Chartered Librarians. Identifies areas in library work for chartered librarian. Proposes a model for an Institution of Chartered Librarians (India).

GUY, RANDOR 185

The high priest of library science, *The Hindu*, New Delhi, Sunday, Aug 30, 1992, Special features, B.

Narrates the biography of Dr S R Ranganathan who was born in a Brahmin family of Tamil Nadu. Describes him as a popular teacher after his scholastic career in Madras, and taking up the job of Madras University Librarian. Discusses his so journ to England, his contribution to the cause of libraries. Recounts his memoirs, his innings at Madras, Banaras Hindu University, Delhi University. Mentions his simple living and simple habits, his sense of humour.

KARAM SINGH 186

Dr S R Ranganathan and his contribution to library science, *RMM*, 59-66.

Gives an account of birth and education of S R Ranganathan, his initiation to the profession of librarianship.

Discusses his contribution as a teacher and writer on classification, cataloguing, organization, book selection, reference service, scientific library administration and management, professional education. Describes national and international recognition of Ranganathan. Discusses about the international conferences held on Ranganathan.

LANGRIDGE, D W 187

Unified vision of library science (Development of Library Science, 2), *Lib Sci slant Docum & Inf Std* 29 (2) June 1992: 91-97.

Review of *Library Science Today* (1965), edited by P N Kaula, reprinted from *Lib Sci slant Docum* 3 (2) June 1966: 101-113. Points out that wholeness in the life and work of S R Ranganathan, stemming from the spiritual foundations of scholarship and learning presented in Indian tradition. Describes his art, discovery and humour, his application of scientific method to librarianship, his pioneering research in library science, his method of teaching, i ntegrations of theory and practice, unification of library science by Five Laws, his approach to classification, etc. Emphasises that essays under review highlight the holistic approach of Indian librarianship.

PANDURANGAM, S 188

The man who enriched library science, *IPLA Souvenir*, 1992. 2p.

Discusses about the achievements of Ranganathan and his contribution to the enrichment of library science by voluminous writings, developing and organising libraries, establishing library associations, opening library education schools, drafting library bills for enactmnet as library acts, etc.

RAMOLA, K C 189

A massiah for the library profession, In *Souvenir* of CLA, 1992.

Describes the birth, education and appointment of S R Ranganthan as librarian of the University of Madras. Discusses his activities and achievements as librarian. Discusses his contribution to the library profession in the form of writings such as his Five Laws of Library Science, Colon Classification, Prolegomena to Library Classification, and others. Explains his contribution to the profession of librairanship as a massiah.

RANGANATHAN on distinctive mission of Indian librarianship for vitalising library service, *In* G L Trehan and Girja Kumar: *Ranganathan Birth Centenary Monograph*, Chandigarh: Chandigarh Library Study Circle, 1993, *pp* 14.a-14.b. 190

Reproduces the distinctive mission of Indian librarianship as given by Dr S R Ranganathana after India's independence and advised the librarians to activate their inner spirit to vitalise the library service to users.

RANGANATHAN's call for changeover to new idèas for dynamic library service: Changing environment, new concepts and new ideas, *In* G L Trehan and Girja Kumar: *Ranganathan Birth Centenary Monograph*, Chandigarh Library Study Circle, 1993, pp 27-28.

States that in view of the changes in the profession, librarians must inculcate new ideas and change their outlook to serve their readers better for a better tomorrow.

RANGRA, V K 192

Ranganathan - apostle of librarianship, *DESIDOC Bull* 12 (5) Sept 1992: 7-12.

Focuses attention on the human aspect of the personality of Ranganathan. Describes his entry into the profession and problems he faced in it. Gives briefly his contributions and achievement. Traces his leanings towards spriritualism and mysticism and their influence on his work. Comments on his style in writing and public speaking. Pleads that to pay a befitting homage to him in the Centenary Year, Ranganathan be posthumously honoured with the highest Republic Day Award.

SATIJA, M P 193

Ranganathan practitioner, *RILISAR Bull* 8 (1) Jan-Mar 1993: 4-25.

Describes in detail the manipulation of laws and certain special normative principles (derived from Five Laws of Library Science) to develop work in the various branches of library and information science. Discusses the methodology of classification, cataloguing, chain indexing, book selection, physical bibliography, and methodology of research in library administration.

VASHISHTH, C P 194

Advancement of librarianship in India, *Jl Lib Inf Sci* 17 (1) June 1992: 102-112.

Mentions early public libraries, establishement of National libraries in India. Enumerates national documentation centres. Discusses library/information infrastructure. Mentions about information services provided at the national level. Discusses public library system. Describes roles of professional associations at the national level. Describes briefly library and information science education. Mentions about school libraries including their standards.

RANGANATHAN'S CONTRIBUTION TO COMPARATIVE LIBRARIANSHIP

KAULA, P N, KRISHAN KUMAR etc, *Eds* 195

International and comparative librarianship and information system: Ranganathan Memorial volumes, 2 volumes, New Delhi, 1994.

Brought out as the Centenary Volumes in two parts it contains 86 papers from 21 countries in commemoration of the work and contribution of Dr S R Ranganathan on his 101st Birth anniversary. Pays tributes to the great Indian librarian and library educator, who has been called by the Amercian Library Association as the 'Father of Information Sciences.'

SEWA SINGH 196

Comparative librarianship and Ranganathan's writings, *Her Lib Sci* 32 (1-2) Jan-Apr 1993: 29-33.

States the emergence of comparative librarianship as a new development in the study of library and information science outside India. Refers to the work of Ranganathan and teaching methodology involving comparative analysis and study. Discusses his work in comparative classification, comparative cataloguing, comparative library services, comparative library legislation, comparative library development programmes and plans. Mentions his work for development of library system for India to achieve "free book service for all".

SEWA SINGH 197

Ranganathan's contribution to the development of comparative librarianship, *RMM*, 19-25B.

Provides definitions of comparative librarianship. Describes the contributions of the Indian writers to comparative librarianship. Discusses in detail the contribution of Ranganathan, among Indian authors, to comparative librarianship, particularly in the fields of classification, cataloguing, library services, library legislation, library development programme. Sums up with his last wish to enact library law for India so that it could have free book service for all the readers.

FIVE LAWS OF LIBRARY SCIENCE

BARMAN, RAJNI KANTA 198

University library development in Assam: A study in the context of Fifth Law of Library Science, *In* C P

Vashishth (Ed), *Library movement and library development in India*: Seminar papers: Thirty-ninth All india Library Conference, Dept of Public Libraries, Govt of Karnataka, Bangalore, January 7-10, 1994, Delhi: Indian Library Association, 1994, pp 284-297.

Discusses the development of higher education in Assam including Gauhati University, Dibrugarh University, Assam Agricultural University. Explains the role of university library in the development of society, education and research. Describes the relevance of Fifth Law of Library Science. Throws light on multifarious growth of the different organs of the libraries attached to the three universities during the period 1970-1992. Discusses their growth in terms of collection, personnel, readers, space, finances, services offered.

BEDI, RAJINDER 199

The father of present libraries, In *Souvenir* of CLA, 1992.

Describes that Dr S R Ranganathan's Five Laws of Library Science are the basis of library science, and on the basis of his contribution of Five Laws only, he can be called as the father of present libraries.

COCHARANE, PAULINE A 200

Information technology in libraries and Ranganthan's Five Laws of Library Science, *Libri* 42 (3) July-Sept 1992: 235-241.

Defines information technology (IT). Discusses that Ranganthan's five Laws can serve as useful guideline and criteria for assessing IT's value in libraries and information services. Indentifies advantages of IT if sensibly used in libraries. Concludes that IT should be used in libraries to provide reference, referral and other services, as well as automating library operations.

FAROOQUI, FARHANA 201

Induction of Five Laws of Library Science in the National Library, Calcutta, *RAT*, 50-53.

States that the Five Laws of Library Science are the basic philosophy behind the existence of the libraries, their services and characteristics. Describes the Five Laws and their induction in activities of the National Library (of India), Calcutta. Concludes that the National Library has been functioning in true confirmity with the Five Laws of Library Science.

FIGUEIREDO, N M d 202

A modernidade des cinco leis de Ranganathan (The currency of Five Laws of Ranganathan), *Ciencia da Informacao* 21 (3) Sept-Dec 1992: 186-191.

Demonstrates the currency of Five Laws of Library Science which can still be used in the establishment of a philosophy of library science as a guideline for the efficient performance of library services and as essential elements in the planning and evaluation of services and information systems at any level.

GOPINATH, M A 203

Public relation in libraries, five laws and library civics, *DL*, 298-306.

Discusses the importance of public relations in libraries. Describes the suggestion of the Five Laws of Library Science to commend public relations as a service. Gives the public relations activity, functions, media and some public relations activity in libraries, such as knowing the readers, advertising library and information products, active interaction, etc. Puts forth also Ranganathan's views on the subject.

JAIN, A C 204

Asymmetical relationship between resource crunch and the Fifth Laws of Library Science, *CLIS Observer* 11 (1-2) Jan-June 1994: 42-46.

States that the Fifth Law of Library Science assumes library as growing and that it has sufficient funds, but contrary to it university libraries in India are facing financial crunch which has hampered the flow of information. Observes that libraries should try to optimise use of their available resources through adoption of certain measures, as resource sharing, use of information technology, etc.

JAMAL, NAYYER 205

Computer: Saves the time of the readers: Its relevance to S R Ranganthan's Fourth Law, *RAT*, 54-57.

Discusses the various activities of a library such as acquisition, cataloguing, circulation, current awareness services, selective dissemination of information, indexing, etc which can be adopted to save the time of the readers as well as staff by using computer. States that similarly other activities such as reference service for which the use of computer can provide the services to the readers without wasting their time.

JAYARAJAN, P 206

The increasing relevance of the Five Laws of Ranganathan, *DESIDOC Bull* 12 (5) Sept 1992: 21-23.

Describes Five Laws of Library Science as the most seminal contribution of Dr S R Ranganathan to librarianship which have more relevance today. Mentions the message of Five Laws focussing on the user which transformed the Indian libraries and the profession. Comments that Ranganathan had high expectations from younger generations of librarians.

KULDIP CHAND and GIAN SINGH 207

Impact of information technology in Ranganathan's Five Laws, *PP,* 21-26.

Lists the Five Laws of Library Science as given by Dr S R Ranganathan. Defines information technology (IT). Examines the impact of IT on all the Five Laws substituting 'Book' with 'Information'. Concludes that new IT will create two classes-those who can pay, and those who can not pay for searching databases.

MUKHOPADHYAY, KABITA 208

Ranganathan's Five Laws of Library Science and its practical implementation, *College Lib* 8 (1-2) 1992 : 17-21.

Describes the Five Laws of Library Science developed and published by Dr S R Ranganathan in 1931 which are the fundamental contribution giving principles and techniques for the proper functioning and management of libraries based on scientific principles. Explains the Five Laws, one by one, for this purpose. Concludes by inspiring the librarians to take an oath in the Birth Centenary Year of Ranganthan to make the library of the readers, for the readers, and by the readers.

NAGARAJAN, M 209

Five Laws of library science-foundation for quality service, *DL* 238-246.

Traces the origin of Five Laws of Library Science of S R Ranganathan. Explains in detail the Five Laws one by one which helped to analyse the various activities and services in libraries, and made the libraries to meet the recreational, informative, educative, and inspirational needs of the modern society. Concludes that in the rapidly developing twentieth century the impact of Five Laws in libraries is unmeasurable.

SHARMA, RAVINDRA N 210

Books are for use: Ranganathan Centennial year, *College & Res News* 8, May 1992: 502.

Describes Ranganathan's Five Laws of Library Science as his work of seminal value. Discusses about the First Law of Library Science: "Books are for Use" in the present context of changes and developments taking place in technology, in book and other formats of reading materials, etc.

SURATI, DAKSHA VINOD 211

Ranganthan's Fourth Law of Library Science and communications revolution, *LIS*, 65-72.

Define. communication and discusses in relation to the Fourth Laws of Ranganathan. Traces development of communication media in human history prior to 1948 and afterwards also as the new communication era in which emphasis is made on electronic communication, microelectronics in communication, telecommunication, etc. where library need to transform itself in an 'Information Agency'.

VISWANATHAN, T 212

Library as growing organism, *Lib Sci slant Docum & Inf Std* 29 (3) Sept 1992: 135-138.

Delivered as a Ranganathan Centenary Lecture at the Documentation Research and Training Centre, Bangalore on 9th August, 1992. Looks at the validity of the Fifth Law of Library Science in the context of advancements in modern technology and their impact on libraries. Explains that the use of CD-ROMs in place of conventional books is visualised. Explains the problems and prospects of CD-ROMs.

VISWANATHAN, T 213

A reflection on Dr Ranganathan's Fifth Law, *Ann Lib Sci & Docum* 39 (2) June 1992: iii-v.

Points out Ranganathan's contribution to library and information science. Mentions the Five Laws of Library Science created by him. Explains the Fifth Law 'Library is a Growing Organism'; the two types of growth. Describes the impact of information technology (IT) on the ways libraries grow in the future. Discusses about electronic library with CD-ROMs. Mentions its inherent problems also. Mentions about the problems of use, classifying CD-ROMs, publishers role, etc. Discusses about the telelibrary which may function much the same way as telephone exchanges linking it with other libraries, and making the entire world as one, which is like today's network.

VOHRA, RANJANA 214

Ranganthan: A trendsetter, In *Souvenir* of CLA, 1992.

Describes S R Ranganathan as one-man library movement. Explains his variegated contributions to the profession, particularly the Five Laws of Library Science through which he enunciated the philosophy of librarianship. Pays tribute to him in this Centenneial year.

WEERASOORIYA, W A 215

Five Laws of Library Science: A philosophical perspective, and their farreaching implications and extensions, *Lib Sci slant Docum & Inft* Std 29 (2) June 1992: 77-84.

Discusses the integral nature of S R Ranganthan's Five Laws of Library Science. Develops the implications of the Five Laws to library networking and delineates a program of action for the network. Emphasises that Five Laws are of immense potential in many fields such as education, political science, besides in library and information science.

RANGANATHAN AND KNOWLEDGE ORGANIZATION

BINWAL, J C 216

Modes of formation of subjects : A model for knowledge representation, *Jl Lib & Inf Sci* 17(1) June 1992: 82-88.

Discusses the concept of social knowledge. Describes the criterion for distinguishing different kinds of social knowledge. Enumerates the attributes of a subject and concept of formation of subjects. Describes empirical study carried out to test the model prepared by S R Ranganathan. Concludes that this model is a powerful tool for knowledge representation in information retrieval.

BINWAL, J C 217

Ranganathan and the universe of knowledge, *Int Classif* 19 (4) 1992: 195-200.

States that S R Ranganathan was the first library and information scientist to recognise the role of developmental and structural studies of subjects in knowledge representation. Mentions structural contribution of Ranganathan. Gives different types of social knowledge. Highlights other structural and developmental attributes of the universe of subjects as propounded by Ranganathan. Points out their relevance and role in information retrieval.

GOPINATH, M A 218

Ranganthan's approach to knowledge organisation its impact on modern library and information services, *Ann Lib Sci & Docum* 39 (2) June 1992: 52-61.

Analyses basic approach to knowledge organisation. Idenetifies the basis of analytico-synthetic approach. Delineates this approach in respect to information seeking, information science, information resources management and information dissemination and retrieval. Leads to the professional expertise in knowledge base communication and education for the same.

INGWERSEN, PETER and WORMELL, IRENE 219

Ranganathan in the perspective of advanced information retrieval, *Libri* 42 (3) July- Sept 1992: 184-201.

Examines S R Ranganthan's approach to knowledge organisation and its relevance to "intellectual accessibility" in libraries . Discusses current and future development of his methodology and theories in knowledge- based system. Elaborates usefulness and applications of analytico-synthetic methodology and establishes parallel with case-frame theory in techniques of information retrieval. Concludes that his helpful sequence and other methodology may have limitation in other fields, but in cognitive modelling his principles for knowledge organisation and faceted methodology find applications.

NEELAMEGHAN, A, GOPINATH,M A, RAGHAVAN,K S and SANKRALINGAM, P , *Eds* 220

Cognitive paradigms in knowledge organisation; Second International ISKO Conference, Bangalore: Sarada Ranganathan Endowment for Library Science, 1992.466p.

Contains 38 papers divided into eight sessions, presented and discussed at the Second International ISKO Conference held at Madras (the first place of work of Ranganathan) during 26-28 August,1992 as part of the Birth Centenary celebrations of Dr S R Ranganathan. It was organised by Madras Library Association, Sarada Ranganathan Endowment for Library Science, and University of Madras. It is published under the ' Ranganathan Centenary Series'.

RANGANTHAN AND COMMUNICATION

SATIJA,M A 221

Communication and Ranganathan, *Int Lib Move* 14 (2) June 1992: 73-78.

Stresses the need of communication. Describes S R Ranganathan's contribution in communication of ideas though his various writings divided into four kinds: Seminal standard: Research standard: Non- specialist standard: and Elementary standard. Mentions his contribution to library and information science journals, series, etc.

RANGANTHAN AND TERMINOLOGY

SATIJA, M P 222

Term-concept relation : A case study of Ranganathan's approach, *In* A Neelamegham, M A Gopinath, et al (Eds), *Cognitive paradigms in knowledge organisation*, Bangalore: Sarada Ranganathan Endowment for Library Science, 1992, pp 460-466.

States that communication is possible through standard terminology, as it is the subtle body of the subject. Explains Ranganathan's contribution to the development of terminology which made it a bedrock of the Indian school of thought. Discusses his work in inter-lingual terminology. Lists his principles for coining new terms and gives his method.

RAGANATHAN AND LIBRARY & INFORMATION SCIENCE EDUCATION

KUMAR, P S G 223

Teaching techniques of Ranganathan, *RMM*, 16-18.

Describes the teaching techniques and methodology of S R Ranganathan which primarily was library-centered. Deals with his techniques of knowing the students, discussing during morning walks. Discusses his classroom method of collective thinking, discussion, anecdotes and analogies, polarisation, etc. Concludes that Ranganathan was a 'Master Educator'.

RAGANATHAN, S R 224

Training of special librarians and imported confusion number two, *IASLIC Bull* 37 (3) Sept 1992: 119-127.

Reprinted from *IASLIC Bulletin* Vol 2 (1-2) December 1957: 32-38, in view of its relevance, under the heading 'Thus wrote Ranganathan'. Points out the gap in the West between the public librarians and special librarians. States that UK is attempting to integrate the public and special librarians. Discusses the position in India which is just the opposite. The training for the two is already integrated with the necessary differentiation at appropriate points. Suggests a plan for strengthening this integrated course and avoiding dissipation.

RANGANATHAN AND RESEARCH

IBRAHIM, ABBAS 225

Ranganathan Institute of Library and Information Science for Applied Research (RILISAR): Developments in MIS for record management/ library automataion & information technology, *RILISAR Bull* 8 (1) Jan 1993: 26-28.

Describes the need of MIS for automation of record management/library and information handling for which are needed specialists in IT in this new information age. Mentions about good career progression in this area for which a course is being initiated by RILISAR from April 1993.

OHDEDAR, A K 226

Study and research on Ranganathan, *IASLIC Bull* 37 (3) Sept 1992: 145-153.

Suggests the possible means of research and study on Ranganathan in three broad directions : (i) Ranganathan's works; (ii) his career activities and achievements; (iii) his life and personality. Suggests the use of published and unpublished sources including sources of oral history. Suggests creation of "Ranganathan Research Library" where all relevant sources be collected for the purpose. Enumerates possible categories of sources and lists already available sources. Hints at a few specific research problems.

SATIJA, M P 227

Ranganathan and team research, *Her Lib Sci* 32 (1-2) Jan-Apr 1993: 11- 17.

States the advantage of collective thinking and research. Gives examples of collaborative work initiated by Ranganathan. Discusses Ranganathan's work through research like Classification Research Group (London), Library Research Circle, Delhi, in association with students and associates. Refers to his writing work, etc and faith in learning through discussion.

SATIJA, M P 228

Ranganathan and team research, *DL*, 59-68.

Describes the team work in librarianship and Ranganathan's contribution to it by involving more professionals in various activities, starting of study circles as Library Research Circle, Delhi, consultation with colleagues, etc to promote team research.

SATIJA, M P 229

Research in librarianship before and after Ranganthan: An overview, *PP*, 27-45.

Traces history of libraries through the ages. Discusses story of research in librarianship in other countries as well as in India. Explains the period of research in library and information science after Ranganathan emerged on the scene, particularly its establishment at the University of Delhi.

SEETHARAMA, S 230

Ranganathan, the methodologist, par excellence, *DL*, 69-80.

Looks at Ranganathan and his contributions from a different angle or perspective, and discusses him as methodologist par excellence. Discusses his methodologies as spiral of scientific method, planes of work, postulational approach, depth classification design, reference service, cataloguing, planning, job analysis, etc.

LIBRARIES AND LIBRARY MOVEMENT

GHANI, MD USMAN 231

Dr S R Ranganathan's contribution to library movement in India, *RAT*, 10-15.

Describes about the Indian library scene at the time of Ranganathan's entry into profession of librarianship and the background in which he worked from Madras, the initial library workshop. Discusses his contribution to education and research, Five Laws, library classification, cataloguing, AACR, his work at Delhi, INSDOC, Banaras Hindu University, Bangalore, activities at government level, his contribution to the National Library, thus creating library movement in the country.

MADRAS LIBRARY ASSOCIATION, MADRAS 232

The library movement: A collection of essays by diverse hands, Madras: Madras Library Association, 1929: Reprinted by Government Press, 1992.

Includes essays on library movement divided in five Sections: English (52 articles): Tamil (9 articles): Canarese (6 articles): and Malyalam (9 articles). Includes also various messages including the one from His Excellency the Right Honourable Viscount Goschen of Hawkhurst, and a Foreword by the Rt. Hon.V S Srinivasa Sastry. The Reprint includes a preface by Dr Suseela Kumar, the present President of Madras Library Association.

RAVI, N, *Ed* 233

The Hindu speaks on libraries, Madras: Kasturi & Sons Ltd, 1992. xvi, 303 p.

Includes the selection of news, views, editorials, etc on libraries covering the period 1918 to 1992 for the benefit of librarians and information scientists. Gives a general view of the development in this field over the past seven decades and a half. Arranged in chronological order covering about 150 items of interest. Pays homage to Dr S R Ranganathan on his Birth Centenary year by publishing this book of interest which also speaks of the library movement in India.

LIBRARY MANAGEMENT

BAKEWELL, K G B 234

Ranganathan library management, *PP*, 101-107.

Discusses S R Ranganathan's contrubution to library management which was scientific in nature for effective management of libraries through his Five Laws of Library Science, book selecttion, reorganisation, communication, classification, etc. States that Ranganathan was way ahead of his contemporaries in this area.

NEELAMEGHAN, A 235

Dimensions in information management: Ranganathan revisited, *Lib Sci slant Docum & Inf Std* 29 (4) Dec 1992: 169-182.

Observes that the developments in information technology, understanding of the role of information in policy and decision-making, problem-solving, system-building,and in socio-economic and political developments have given new lease of life to the Fifth Law of Library Science. Defines information resource management. Covers transformations that are happening in physical media for information, in particular, the telematic access, the development of varieaty of computer based meagneto-laser-optico databases, and the emergence of information utilisation culture towards human societal development.

INFORMTION RETRIEVAL

HASHMI, ABUZAR 236

Ranganathan on non-conventional methods in document retrieval, *RAT*, 44-49.

Describes about the introduction of the non-conventional methods in informaation retrieval in the second half of twentieth century. Discusses only application of computers in document retrieval and contribution of Ranganathan in computerised information retrieval, Colon Classification, and the computer CIRS in National Library of India and role of Ranganathan. Mentions about the databases developed in the National Library and the future plans.

RANGANATHAN AND INFORMATION TECHNOLOGY

MISHRA, S, JOSHI, M K and MISRA, M K 237

Relevance of Ranganathan's contribution in the age of information technology, *Ann Lib Sci & Docum* 39 (2) June 1992: 69-71.

Studies Ranganathan's ideas and philosophy revealing some amazing concepts which have the potential to solve the complexities of the present system. Discusses the relevance of the Five Laws, information organization, and retrieval, bibliographic record formats in the context of computer and communication technologies. Concludes that Ranganathan's ideas are seminal in nature and need careful attention from the professionals, academicians and researchers.

VASHISHATH,C P ,*Ed* 238

Library and information technology: In pursuit of excellence: Seminar papers of 38th All India Library Conference of ILA, Delhi: Indian Library Association, 1992. 318p.

Contains 43 articles divided into six Sections according to the theme of the Conference of the Indian Library Association held at Bhubneswar during 21-24 November 1992. The publication has been brought out with salutations to the Father of Library Science in India on his 101st birthday being celebrated all over the world.

BIBLOGRAPHIC CONTROL

RAMAIAH, L S and KANKACHRY, M, *Eds* 239

Documentation and bibliogrphic control of the humanities in India, New Delhi: Aditya Prakashan, 1992. xv, 349.

It is dedicated to Padamshri SR Raganathan in his centenary year. With a Foreward by P N Kaula, discusses the present position of the humanties, their importance and the state of their bibliographic control. Includes 33 papers divided into 8 sections relating to the importnace of the humanities, classification for humanities, problems and prospects, research activity, tools for bibliorgaphic control, insititutional profiles, and bibliographic control proposals.

PRE-NATAL CATALOGUING

LAXMAN RAO, N and PRAFULLA CHANDRA, T V 240

Ranganathan's concept of pre-natal cataloguing: A precursor to cataloguing-in-publication, *IJILIS* 5 (3-4) July-Dec 1992: 258-265.

States that the concept of centralised cataloguing became popular after Ranganathan propounded his ideas on pre-natal cataloguing and resulted ultimately in the present Cataloguing-in-Publication, and now Cataloguing-in-Source. Discusses its implications on ISBN, CIS, CIP. Concludes with the suggestion that in the Birth Centenary year of Ranganathan, CIP should be introduced for Indian publications in various disciplines and languages.

COPARATIVE STUDY OF AACR AND CCC

CHOUDHURY, BIJOY KUMAR and MISHRA, SANJAYA 241

Government as author: Treatment in CCC and AACR 2, 1988 revision, *Her Lib Sci* 30 (3-4) July-Oct 1991: 205-211.

Discusses various types of government publications. Attempts a critical analysis of the treatment of rules in CCC-Edition 5 and AACR-2, 1988 revision. Brings out similarities and dissimilarities in rendering of various types of government publications with examples according to both the Codes.

CHOUDHURY, BIJOY KUMAR and MOHANTA, RABINDRA NATH 242

Institution as author: A comparative study of CCC and AACR 2, *Luck Libn* 22 (1-2) Mar-June 1990: 6-12.

Enumerates the relevant rules of CCC-Ed 5 with amendments and AACR-2 (1988) in the choice of heading and rendering of different types of institutions with suitable examples. Compares the rules to bring out similarities and dissimilarities in the treatment of institutions at the level of its definition and cases of conflict in both the Codes.

CHOUDHURY, BIJOY KUMAR, RAUT, B and PADHEE, B K 243

Pseudonymous works: Comparative study of CCC 5th Edition (with amendments) and AACR 2, 1988 revision, *Her Lib Sci* 29 (3-4) July-Oct 1990: 213-220.

Defines pseudonym according to CCC and AACR-2, gives its types. Discusses treatment of relevant rules in both the codes. Points out similarities and dissimilarities with regard to rules for choice and rendeing of *pseud.* Suggests that criteria should be the name popularly established in literary world.

CHAIN INDEXING / INDEXING

BATTY,C D 244

The influence of Ranganathan on the structural design of index languages, *PP*, 47-59.

Traces the origin of classification from Aristotle to Dewey. Discusses the beginnings of synthesis in classification from Dewey. Describes in detail the contribution of Ranganathan to the discipline of classificaation. Discusses Ranganathan's development of facet analysis. Explains Ranganathan's fundamental contribution to classification in England and the USA. Mentions also about Artifical Intelligence systems.

GOPINATH, M A 245

Chain index and its impact on subject indexing, *Lib Sci slant Docum & Inf Std* 26 (3) Sept 1990s 167-185.

Analyses the basis of Ranganathan's chain indexing and its values in the systematic subject index to information retrieval. Discusses impact of hierarchical chain in the formation of chain in POPSI and PRECIS.The current approaches to on line search strategies stimulate the formation of .chain in subject heading formulations.

VICKERY, B C 246

Ranganathan's contribution to indexing, *SRR*, 8-10.

Describes the background when Ranganathan gave his ideas on indexing. Discusses that his ideas have penetrated the theory and practice of indexing in the form of the principle of synthesis, the principle of symbiosis between classification and cataloguing or index.

BOOK NUMBERS

MISHRA, SANJAYA 247

Colon Book Number, *Luck Libn* 22 (3-4) Sept - Dec 1990: 80-88.

Discusses meaning,need, purpose and history of book numbers. Explains Ranganathan's book numbering system. Cites some problems in Colon Book Number and gives their solutions also. Concludes that Colon Book Number is the best of all the book numbering systems available.

SATIJA,M P and AGRAWAL,S P 248

Book number in the new Edition, *CC*, 131-140.

Describes the book numbering system as followed in Colon Classification of Ranganathan. Points out problems arising out of this system. Mentions some of the advantages of this book number developed by Ranganathan.

SATIJA, M P and AGRAWAL, S P 249

Book numbers:Some Indian methods, New Delhi: Concept Publishing Company, 1990. 96p.

Divided into four chapters covering Book numbers-what and why; Ranganathan and his system; two other Book number systems; Collection number and call number. Describes their advantages and disadvantages. Also includes two Appendices.

SATIJA, M P and COMAROMI, JOHN P 250

Beyond classification: Book numbers, New Delhi: Ess Ess Publications, 1992. 115p.

Discusses about the various Book numbering systems available at present. Defines book numbers, and gives their history. Favours chronological book numbers and gives their advantages. Ends with a chronology of book numbers and a useful bibliography.

CLASSIFICATION THEORY

AMAN, MOHAMMED M 251

Ranganathan the classificationist, *RAW*, 1-9.

Describes the importance of the Five Laws of Ranganathan which had international appeal. Discusses in detail his contribution to classification, to terminology, development of scientific method, theories, deep analysis and synthesis, etc. Describes his Colon Classification, contribution to facet analysis, contribution to cataloguing. Concludes that he had international impact as a classificationist and true library scientist.

BATTY, C D 252

The influenece of Ranganathan on the structural design of index languages, *PP*, 47-59.

Traces the origins of classification from Aristotle to Melvil Dewey. Discusses the beginnings of systhesis in classification from Dewey. Describes in detail the contribution of Ranganathan to the discipline of classification. Discusses Ranganathan's development of fact analysis. Explains Ranganathan's fundamental contribution to classification in England and the USA. Mentions also about Artificial Intelligence systems.

CURRAS, EMILIA 253

Ranganathan's classification theories under the systems science postulates, *Jl Lib & Inf Sci* 17 (1) June 1992: 45-65.

Describes the basic ideas about systems science. Discusses Ranganathan's ideas about concept of 'universe of ideas', 'universe of science', 'universe of knowledge', 'universe of classification'. Examines principles, canons and postulates underlying Colon Classification. Discusses structure of Colon Classification. Points out that the ideas of Ranganathan conform to the concept of 'unity of science'. Concludes that the principles of systems science or system thinking are helpful in understanding theory of classification.

GOPINATH, M A 254

General systems theory vis-a-vis classification theory of Ranganathan, *CPT*, 114-121.

Discusses general systems theory and its laws. Highlights application of these laws to the development of a theory of classification. Evaluates research done in classification in India and Britain. Redefines PMEST in terms of systems theory. Formulates rules on the basis of principles derived from systems law for the development of schedules for classification and procedures for classifying of documents for collection formation.

GOPINATH, M A 255

Science of classification: Ranaganathan's contribution to classification, *Jl Lib & Sci Inf* 17 (1) June 1992: 66-70.

Indentifies the contribution of Ranaganathan towards scientific basis for classification. Discusses the values in developing theory and practice of classification in the current day inter-disciplinary subjects in library and information science.

GOPINATH, M A 256

Towards a scientific approach to classification and cataloguing: Contributions of SR Ranganathan, *Lib Sci slant Dosum & Inf Std* 29 (2) June 1992: 85-89.

States that development of scientific approach to classification and cataloguing were initiated by S R Ranganathan. He provided a theoretical framework for the development of these intensely practical techniques in library science. Points out that such theoretical framework in the form of a hierarchy of normative principles are capable of guiding the contextual situations arising out of the new developments in the field of library and information services.

KAWAMURA, K 257

Current problems in classification and indexing: Inferences drawn from observations of some British expertises linked to the thoughts of Ranganathan, *T P & D Forum Series* (Japanese), 1, 1992: 28-52.

Describes about the current problems being faced and discussed all over in the field of classification and indexing. Deals with the inferences drawn from the British experts which have further been linked to the thoughts and ideas of Dr S R Ranganathan who put forward many seminal ideas in classification.

KRISHAN KUMAR 258

Distinctive contribution of Ranganathan to library classification, *Jl Lib & Inf Sci* 17 (2) Dec 1992: 116-127.

Discusses Ranganathan's distinctive contribution to library classification such as normative principles, three planes model of work,freely facted classification, postulational approach, Fundamental categories, certain notational devices like sector device, group notation device, emptying digit device, and seminal mnemonic device. Considers 7th Edition of Colon Classification as the best example of application of all these ideas of the truly great scholar.

KUMAR, P S G 259

Ranganathan through classification, *PP*, 1-5.

Attempts to throw light on Ranganathan's qualities through classification approach in that looking at his universe of knowledge, his attributes, his characteristics, his arrays and chains, and phases and facets, and fundamental categories, in terms of life span, space, etc.

LANGRIDGE, D W 260

My debt to Ranaganthan, *PP*, 7-11.

Describes author's meetings and discussions with Ranganathan particularly on classification, among others. Discusses about the benefits derived from Ranganathan's work and contribution in classification. Pays tribute to Dr S R Ranganathan during the Birth Centenary celebrations and expresses his debt to the great man.

McILWAINE, I C 261

Ranganathan and classification in Britain, *PP*, 93-100.

Speaks of Ranganathan's days at the School of Library, Archives and Information Studies at the University College, London in 1924-25. Discusses about the papers Ranganathan wrote in examinations and the score he got, the teaching methods followed then. Discusses about Ranganathan's contribution in classification and his influence in Britain particularly through Classification Research Group (UK).

NARANG, S P 262

Some theoretical innovations by Dr S R Ranganathan in classification, cataloguing and indexing: An overview, *RMM*, 50-58.

Explains in detail to give an account of Ranganathan's theoretical innovations particularly in classification, cataloguing and indexing which provide a scientific base for the revolutionary information technology using computeised systems for information analysis, storage and retrieval.

OKKO, M 263

Ranganathan in trend on kasuum malleitaja kasitteellisten lainojm ymmarrettavyydesta (Ranganathan's models for the growth of knowledge and on comprehensibility of borrowed concepts), *Kirjastotiedga* 11 (2) 1992: 53-60.

Discusses about the models given by S R Ranganathan for the growth of knowledge, his contribution to classification and the classificatory concepts he used in his theoretical framework.

RAJU, A A N 264

Ranganathan: The propounder of dynamic theory of library classification, *DL*, 81-87.

Explains the emergence of dynamic theory of classification and the basic work of S R Ranganathan. Gives its ingredients, normative principles, impact of dynamic theory of Ranganathan on Dorking Conference held in 1957, on British Classification Research Group, on American students, etc.

RAJU, A A N 265

Ranganathan: The propounder of dynamic theory of subject classificataion, *Her Lib Sci* 32 (1-2) Jan-Apr 1993: 17-21.

States the early work on classification through descriptive theory. Describes early emergence and application of dynamic theory of classification propounded by Ranganathan. Discusses the basic work on dynamic theory through the work of Classification Research Group (UK), and through the outcome of Dorking Conference.

RANGANATHAN and classification: A chronology, 266

1924-1992, *CC*, 194-205.

Provides in chronological order, the conception and developments of Colon Classification of Dr S R Ranganathan. Puts the chronology for the benefit of the readers, in an Appendix-A.

SATIJA, M P 267

Classification and indexing in India. A state-of-the-art, In *Papers*, 58th IFLA General Conference, New Delhi, 30 Aug - 5 Sept 1992: 4.26- 4.29.

Explains the real beginning with Ranganathan as the mechanism of Colon Classification; his contribution to library and information science. Discusses Documentation Research and Training Centre and Sarada Ranganathan Endowment for Library Science and their contribution to library classification, India's contribution to classification terminology, classification practices in India, classification teaching, research and literature, classification organisation, and conferences on classification.

SATIJA, M P 268

Ranganathan and classificatiton: A chronology 1924-1992: *Int Classif* 19 (1) 1992: 3-6.

Identifies some sources on which is based this chronology giving Ranganathan's development in the field of library classification with short description of the impact and significance of the dates.The chronology which has been structured according to some periods of his life determined mostly by location lists. Mentions also some post mortem events.

SATIJA, M P 269

A deserted bastion: classificaion and indexing in India: a study of art, *Int Cat & Bib Control* 22 (3) July-Dec 1993: 51-54.

Presented at the 58th General Conference of IFLA, New Delhi, 1992, gives short account of Ranganathan. Discusses contribution of DRTC, Sarada Ranganathan Endowment for Library Science. Explains India's contribution to subject cataloguing, classification terminology, classification practices of India. Discusses about classification organisation, and conferences, etc.

SEETHARAMA, S 270

Role of classification in information services generation, *Lib Sci slant Docum & Inf Std* 29 (2) June 1992: 109-118.

Mentions areas of application of the postulates and principles of Ranganathan's general theory of knowledge classification. Indicates that classification in the sense of organising concepts is involved in the generation, storage, retrieval, and dissemination of information, especially in designing databases, construction of user interest profile, subject description of documents, arrangements and presentation of information, etc. Demonstrates with examples, the application of Ranganathan's postulates and principles of classification in the preparation of an information analysis and consolidation procduct.

SVENONIUS, ELAINE 271

Ranganathan and classification science, *Libri* 42 (3) July-Sept 1992: 176-183.

Discusses some of Ranganathan's contribution to the production, practical and theoretical aspects of classification science. These include: (1) a set of design criteria to guide the designing of schemes for knowledge/subject classification; (2) a conceptual framework for organising the universe of subject; and (3) an understanding of the general principles underlying subject disciplines and classification languages. Concludes that Ranganathan has contributed significantly to laying the foundations for a science of subject classification.

XIAO, YAN 272

Modern development of classification: Research and practice in the People's Republic of China, *Int Classif* 19 (1) 1992: 10-14.

Reviews the prospects of modern classification research and practice in China. Gives a systematic description of the evolution in methodology, scope and orientation of classification research with special emphasis being put on the influence of Colon Classification and the principle of facet and analysis and synthesis established by Dr S R Ranganathan.

CLASSIFICATION AND DATABASE DESIGNING

NEELAMEGHAN, A 273

Application of Ranganathan's general theory of knowledge classification in designing specialized databases, *Libri* 42 (3) July-Sept 1992: 202-226.

Discusses some practical applications of the postulates, principles and techniques of Ranganathan within the framework of his general theory of knowledge classification in the design and development of specialized databases. Highlights usefulness of postulational approach, helpful sequence, etc. Illustrates application of mnemonics in designing intergrated databases. States that interaction between system designers and end users is essential to understand user perception of reality and their information requirements.

NEELAMEGHAN, A 274

Application of S R Ranganathan's postulates and principles of the general theory of knowledge classification to database design and information retrieval. In *Papers*, 58th IFLA General Conference, New Delhi,30 Aug-5 Sept 1992, pp 4.20-4.25.

Mentions that Ranganathan's postulates and principles of the general theory of knowledge classification can be applied in structuring knowledge bases and object-oriented databases, designing schemes of classification, vocabulary control tools. Demonstrates enhancement of user-friendliness of information retrieval by interfacing facet analysed query terms with thesaurus terms to the analytico-synthetic freely faceted model.

NEELAMEGHAN, A 275

Application of S R Ranganathan's postulates and principles of the general theory of knowledge classification to databases design and information retrieval, *Int Cat and Biblio Control* 22 (3) July-Sept 1993: 46-50.

Describes Ranganathan's holistic integrative approach. Explains application of analytico-synthetic methodology. Considers this and the related postulates and principles of his General Theory of knowledge classification to the design and development of databases, in particular, specialised and object-oriented databases and in information retreval. Demonstrates improved user- friendliness of information system resulting from interfacing facet-analysed query terms with thesaurus terms.

MODES OF FORMATION OF SUBJECTS

NEELAMEGHAN, A 276

Ranganathan's generalised model of subject structure and modes of formation of subjects, *In* A Neelameghan, M A Gopinath, et al (Eds), *Congnitive paradigms in knowledge organisation*, Bangalore: Sarada Ranganathan Endowment for Library Science, 1992, pp 269-285

Gives working definitions of some concepts, as entity, idea, kniwledge, subject, etc. Recaptulates postulates of modes of formation of subjects. Discusses Ranganathan's conceptual model of subject structure and its usefulness in the organisation of subjects. Reviews the various modes of formation of subjects examined by Ranganathan and his associates and use of the subject areas thus formed in schemes for classification.

FACET ANALYSIS

FOSKETT, D J 277

Ranganathan and "user friendliness", *Libri* 42 (3) July-Sept 1992: 227-234.

Defines ‘user-friendliness’. States that Ranganathan's Five Laws place the user as the focus of library and information services and emphasize the need to understand the user. Describes that facet analysis helps the information specialist to understand and interpret the subject of user’s enquiry which contributes to user-friedilness. Mentions that facet analysis reflects a natural way of thinking and can be introduced into computerized systems.

FRIIS-HANSEN, JENS B 278

Facets and clustres, *PP*, 71-75.

States that Dewey Decimal Classification was established as a shelving system, hence enumerative. Mentions that new concepts of facets etc were developed in Colon Classification of Ranganathan which is the foundation of whole system. Describes faceting as ideal technique for representing subject content, and searching aid. Says that clusters help in information searching particularly in Danish libraries.

GOPINATH, M A 279

Ranganthan’s theory of facet analysis and knowledge representation, *DESIDOC Bull* 12 (5) Sept 1992: 16-20.

Presents the basis of Ranganathan’s theory of facet analysis and identifies its application to the analysis of knowledge. Discusses its value in knowledge representation in different contexts. Gives examples from design database for public finance.

IYER, HEMLATA 280

Facet analysis and information retrieval, *CC*, 116-123.

Deals with the empirical testing of Ranganathan’s facet structure, especially in on-line envronment. Establishes the measure of concreteness of the categories useful in classification.

SEETHARAMA, S 281

Cognitive approach in information consolidation, *In* A Neelameghan, M A Gopinath, et al (Eds) *Cognitivie paradigms in knowledge organisation,* Bangalore: Sarada Ranganathan Endowment for Library Science, 1992, pp 286-292.

Mentions the usefulness of Ranganathan's facet model. Demonstrates with an example how such a cognitive model can be used in information/ knowledge representation in an information consolidation product. Concludes that librarians and information scientists should realise the full implication of Ranganathan's work and apply it for the generation of new information services.

SUKHDEV SINGH 282

Anatomy and physiology of Ranganathan's facet-analysis, *RMM*, 36-43.

Defines facet-analysis. Discusses in detail the contribution of Ranganathan to facet analysis as an approach to library classification. Describes implementation of facet-based retrieval, knowledge representation systems, development of decision support systems for information retrieval whereby classification provides a kind of relational framework for knowledge base systems.

FUNDAMENTAL CATEGORIES

FOSKETT, D J 283

More on the personality facet, *Jl Lib & Inf Sci* 17 (1) June 1992: 39-44.

Mentions use of notational systhesis or number building in different classification schemes. Points out the use of facet analysis by S R Ranganathan is an exact parallel with the central notion of General Systems Theory. Explains that

Ranganathan's concept of 'personality' facet seems to correspond closely with 'whole', 'wholeness' of General Systems Theory. Concludes that none has yet attempted an alternative term to 'personality' which so accurately mirrors the central concept of General Systems Theory.

MNEMONICS

MANDAL, SATYANANDA 284

Seminal mnemonics in classification system and Prof. Ranganathan, *College Lib* 8 (1-2) 1992: 14-16.

Makes an attempt to trace the origin of the concept of seminal mnemonic, a concept which is absent in other classification languages. Discusses Ranganathan's thought about non sensual perception and cognition beyond sense organs. States that as seminal mnemonics has its special flavour in classificatory environment, that Ranganathan discussed Indian philosophy, Indian classics, and tried to assimilate and absorb it into knowledge organising systems.

NOTATION

RANGANATHAN, S R 285

Zone analysis and mixed notation, *IASLIC Bull* 37 (3) Sept 1992: 101-106.

Reproduced from *IASLIC Bulletin* 1 (2) Dec 1956: 44-47, in view of its relevance, under the heading 'Thus wrote Ranganathan'. Gives history of mixed notation with the use of the connecting symbols needed in an analytico-synthetic classification suited to the needs of depth classification. Points out advantages of zone formation in an array, with mixed notation, to accommodate new classes, isolates of a facet, telescoped facet. Points out the vast amount of routine search to be done and the economics of zone analysis.

POSTULATES

IYER, HEMLATA 286

Subject representation and entropy, *Int Classif* 19 (1) 1992: 5-18.

Examines the systems approach to subject structuring. Presents an overview of empirical studies undertaken to test the postulates relating to subject structuring. Discusses Ranganathan's catetgories and absolute syntax. Says that entropy provides a disorganization in a system. Structured subject representation are considered as systems. Studies empirical validation of Ranganathan's postulates, concreteness of categories, bond strength, etc.

COLON CLASSIFICATION

CHATTERJEE, AMITABHA 287

Concept of phase relation in CC and its impact on BC, *IASLIC Bull* 37 (3) Sept 1992: 163-170.

States that though the idea of Phase Relation was first initiated by Universal Decimal Classification, most of the other schemes either ignored or tried by enumeration. Explains that only Ranganathan developed the idea to a finer degree and gave it a concrete shape in his Colon Classification. Mentions that though Bliss followed enumeration in BC-1, but BC-2 adopted analytico- synthetic method for phase relation. Attempts to establish the impact of CC on BC in this regard.

CHATTERJEE, AMITABHA 288

Making of Colon Classification: The inside story, *College Lib* 8 (1-2) 1992: 22-25.

Relates the interesting story as to how the idea of the Colon Classification was first conceived and given shape by S R Ranganathan since 1924. Identifies the various problems he faced during its preparation, and the solutions found by him. States that it helped Ranganathan to lay a strong foundation for the magnificent edifice of the Colon Classification, the most outstanding contribution from his fertile mind.

GIRJA KUMAR 289

Classic classifications, *Frontline* 9 (17) Aug 15-28, 1992: 62.

Gives a brief account about some of the classification schemes deemed to be classics such as those of British Museum, Bibliotheque Nationale (Paris), Dewey Decimal Classification, Libray of Congress Classification, Universal Decimal Classification, and Colon Classification of Dr S R Ranganathan.

GOPINATH, M A 290

Colon Classification: Its theory and practice, *CC*, 68-98.

Presents the developments in PMEST, new developments in Colon Classification as primary Basic Subjects (BS), Systems, Environmented Basic Subjects, Specials, Secondary Basic Subjects, Compound Basic Subjects, Schedules of Common Property isolates, Matter Property isolates, Energy isolates, Space isolates, Language isolates, Phase Relation indicators, Anteriorising Common Isolates (ACI),etc.

MAHAPATRA, M 291

Design of special classification schedules based on the principles of Colon Classification, *CC*, 159-179.

Describes the basic steps required for the design of special classification schedules on the Idea Plane and Verbal Plane, as followed by the Documentation Research Training Centre for designing the depth classification of Colon Classification.

SEHGAL, R L 292

Handbook of Colon classification, New Delhi: Ess Ess Publicatitons, 1993. xii, 296 p.

Deals with the evolution, development and the present state of the Colon Classification system of library classification developed by Dr S R Ranganathan and for which he is known all over. Discusses the theoretical foundations, canons, principles, postulates, categories, facet analysis, etc for the benefit of its users. Gives suitable example wherever needed.

VERMA, JITENDER 293

Colon thesaurus of social science terms, New Delhi: Khanna Publishers, 1992. xv, 150 p.

Describes the methodology of preparing a thesaurus with the principles and theories of Colon Classification of Dr S R Ranganathan. Explains the development of a thesaurus of social science terms with the assistance of Colon Classification.

COLON CLASSIFICATION - BIBLIOGRAPHIES

SATIJA, M P and AMRIK SINGH 294

Bibliography of Colon Classification, 1930-1993 , New Delhi: M D Publicattions, 1994. xi, 129 p.

Includes 1371 entries in this chronologically arragned bibliography. It has 98% of the literaure in English language, and others in Hindi, and other languages. Also covers M L I Sc disserations. Delineates the genesis and development of CC from the beginning todate. Pays tribute to S R Ranganathan on the occasion of his Birth Centenary clebrations world wide.

SEWA SINGH and SUKHBIR SINGH 295

Colon Classification: A select bibliography, New Delhi: Ess Ess Publications, 1992. xvii, 86 p.

Covers 701 entries in this select bibliography on Colon Classification. States that the material has been taken from various primary and secondary sources. Arranged in classified order according to the subject headings such as General Classification, Colon Classification- Edition 7, philosophy, history, features of Colon Classification. More headings include Design, Depth classification, automatic classification, uses of classification, canons, Common Isolates, postulates, Fundamental Categories, and so on. Entries are further arranged in alphabetical order under each heading. Claims not be comprehensive in coverage. Dedicated to the memory of the Great Master Dr S R Ranganathan in his Birth Centenary year.

COLON CLASSIFICATION - EDITION 1

KRISHAN KUMAR 296

Historical roots of Ranganathan's Colon Classification (Edition 1), *Jl Lib & Inf Sci* 17 (1) June 1992: 71-81.

Describes Ranganathan's contribution to library and information science in gneral. Mentions about his library education at London and influence of Berwick Sayers. Describes the seeds of Colon Classification, Edition 1, and its salient features. Brings out Ranganathan's indebtedness to Melvil Dewey, influence of Universal Decimal Classification on Colon Classification- Ed 1. Discusses the growth of the concept of 'categories'. Mentions the influence of Hulme, Biscoe, and others. Concludes that he possessed an amazing degree of ingenuity to apply old ideas so as to look original.

COLON CLASSIFICATION - EDITION 7

ASUNDI, A Y 297

Common isolates in Colon Classification with emphasis on Edition 7, *CC,* 107-115.

Discusses about the common isolates as introduced in Colon Classification right from the beginning, ie, its first edition. Defines common isolates. Gives canons of common isolates, and enumerates changes in common isolates from Edition 1 of Colon Classification to its Edition 7.

CHATTERJEE, AMITABHA and
CHOWDURY, G G 298

CC 7 : An evaluation of its development in three planes, *CC*, 25-67.

Gives a detailed account of Colon Classification - Edition 7 discussing all the salient features, additions made, modifications effected, new concepts incorporated within the purview of the three planes of work as propounded by S R Ranganathan.

DHYANI, P 299

Colon Classification - Edition 7, *CC*, 1-10.

Discusses the structure of Colon Classification made with regard to Language Isolates, Time Isolates, Space Isolates, Phase Relations, special isolates, and notational system. Concludes that publication of CC-7 is a positive development made by the Editor.

KUMAR, P S G 300

Notational developments in tbe CC with special reference to Edition 7, *CC*, 124-130.

Discusses the noatation of Colon Classification of S R Ranganathan with regard to zones in Main Classes of Colon Classification -Edition 6 and Colon Classification -Edition 7. Discusses its other features such as modes of formation of subjects, compound subjects, complex subjects, etc.

NAVANEETHAN, R 301

Implementation of COBOL program for index to the Colon Classification, Edition 7, *DRTC 1990* , pp S 1-12.,

Explains briefly the data structure, organisation, and program development of CCINDEX program for preparing index to the Edition 7 of Colon Classification using COBOL language. Explains development of screens using COBOL screen manager utility.

SATIJA, M P 302

Colon Classification 7th Edition, *ULI*, 123-134.

States that Colon Classification - Edition 7 has made drastic changes. Examines these changes critically. Mentions features of new Edition such as simplification of rules, identification of more Basic Subjects, increase in number and variety of common isolates. Points out demerits. States that 17 Indian universities and 16 colleges use Colon Classificcation. Concludes that the scheme should be kept alive.

SATIJA, M P 303

Colon Classification, 7th Edition, 1966-1991: A literature analysis, *CC*, 206-215.

Provides a literature analysis of what has been published on Colon Classification during 1966-1991. Gives a list of 59 references published during the period of 26 years, with yearly average of 2.27 publications.

SATIJA, M P *Ed* 304

Colon Classification 7th edition: Some perspectives, New Delhi: Sterling Publishers, 1993. xx, 220 p.

Includes 12 essays on the various aspects of Colon Classification - 7th Edition of Dr S R Ranganathan, and edited by M A Gopinath. Covers such topics as descriptive, theoretical, and individual aspects in this publication. Also includes two Appendices including a bibliography on CC-7.

SATIJA, M P 305

Use of Colon Classification, *CC* 180-193.

Gives a brief account of Colon Classification of Ranganathan.Discusses sources for studies on the use of Colon Classification system. Presents some statistics based on these sources. Points out that the future use of Colon Classification is difficult to predict.

SATIJA, M P and GUPTA, O P 306

Colon Classification, 7th Edition (1987) :A concise introduction, *CC*, 99-106.

Provides a brief introduction of the 7th Edition of Colon Classification of Ranganathan, touching all the salient features. Discusses about all other changes made in this new edition of CC.

SETHI, A R 307

CC 7: Some preliminary observations, *CC*, 11-24.

Brings forth the association of Jawaharlal Nehru University Library and Colon Classification - Edititon 7. Presents an evaluative account of CC-7 giving its salient features, changes in three planes of work, Environmental divisions, common isolates, special isolates, etc. Gives examples of adhocism, complexity, etc giving difficulties in its use in Jawaharlal Nehru University Library.

SEWA SINGH 308

A practical manual of Colon Classification: Edition 7, Bombay: JAICO Publishing House, 1991. xii, 305 p.

Includes 49 brief chapters on the practice and theory of Colon Classification, Edition 7 of S R Ranganathan.Part I includes 38 chapters on practical examples, analysis of titles, rules, etc. Part II includes 11 chapters on the threotical aspects of Colon Classification - Edition 7; while in Part III are given answers to Exercises for Practice included in Part I. States that it is primarily written for students of Colon Classification.

SEWA SINGH 309

Time and space isolates in CC-7: A study, *ILA Bull* 27 (4) Jan-Mar 1992: 168-177.

Makes a comparative study of the Space and Time isolates scheldules of Colon Classification Edition 6 and Edition 7. Discusses in detail the Space and Time isolates in the 7th Edition of CC. Opines that provisions of CC-7 have made the numbers and number building process rather complicated and complex by increasing the number of digits in a Class Number.

SHABAHAT HUSSAIN 310

A theoretical basis for the accommodation of new subjects in Colon Classification Edition 7, *CC*, 141-158.

Investigates how Colon Classification Edition 7, with its strong theoretical base, deals with the problem of a growing universe of subjects. Discusses the work in the Idea Plane, formation of new subjects, and work in the Notational Plane to accommodate them suitably.

SOMA RAJU, P 311

Colon Classification on the march: An overview, *DLIS*, 397-408.

Describes the development of Colon Classification through its various editions, particularly its Edition 7. Presents the features of Colon Classification, 7th Edition in conceptual and notational aspects. Points out shortcomings in the Schedules. Makes suggestions to improve it further.

RANGANATHAN's IMPACT ON DDC

DHYANI, P 312

Ranganathan's normative principles and Dewey Decimal Classification, *PP*, 61-69.

Discusses normative principles of Ranganathan and its application to Dewey Decimal Classification because it is being used in 70% of Indian libraries of different types. Explains individualisation of clubbed isolates, Add device, relocations, etc and their usefulness in Dewey Decimal Classification scheme.

COMPARATIVE STUDY OF CC AND DDC

MANDAL, SATYANANDA 313

Geographical area in CC7 and DDC-20: Some observations, *College Libn* 6(1-4) 1990: 3- 7.

Discusses geographical area and its problems in classification. Describes salient features and changes concerning geographical areas in CC Edition 7 and DDC Edition 20. Points out some problems and makes suggestions. Stresses the need of revision and cooperation in this regard.

LIBRAMETRICS / BIBLIOMETRICS / INFORMETRICS

GOPINATH, M A 314

Ranganathan : A profile in relation to librametry, *Her Lib Sci* 32 (1-2) Jan-Apr 1993: 7-11.

Discusses the contribution of S R Ranganathan with emphasis on use and quantitative measures for library operations leading to use of the term "Librametry". Discusses further these quantitative measures in relation to all library operations such as classification, cataloguing, library advertisement, library services, etc.

GOPINATH, M A 315

Shiyali Ramamrita Ranganathan: A profile In relation to librametry *In* Ravichandra Rao (Ed), *Informetrics-91*: selected papers from the Third International Conference on Informetrics, 9-12 August 1991, Bangalore, Bangalore: Sarada Ranganathan Endowment for Library Science, 1992, pp. 9-16.

Discusses Dr S R Ranganathan's contributions with emphasis on use and quantitative measures for library operations leading to the use of the term "Librametry". These quantitative measures are discussed in relations to all library operations such as classifications, cataloguing, library administration, library services, etc.

LANCASTER, F W, ZETER, MARY JO and METZLER, LAURA 316

Ranganathan's influence examined bibliometrically, *Libri* 42 (3) July-Sept 1992: 268-281.

Studies through a bibliometric analysis of the citation to Ranganathan's writings over the period 1956-1990, using *Social Science Citation Index* and *Science Citation Index* that this influence has not diminished over the years. States that his books are more frequently cited than his articles. Mentions that citations to *Prolegomena* (95), Colon Classificatioon (69), Classified Catalogue Code (32), Five Laws (28) account for more than a third of the total of 630 citations.

MAHAPATRA, GAYATRI 317

Post Ranganathan era: A bibliomentric analysis of Ranganathan's contributions, *Iaslic Bull* 37 (3) Sept 1992: 177-182.

Measures degree of influence of Ranganathan's work on Indian library and information science literature by analysing the references provided in the articles of journals. Reveals that Ranganathan's works were highly cited even long after his expiry. States that classification and cataloguing are influenced most by Ranganathan's contributions.

RAVICHANDRA RAO, I K , *Ed* 318

Informetrics 91; selected papers from the Third Informatin Confrence on informetrics, Bangalore: Sarada Ranganathan Endowment for Library Science, 1992. 577 p.

Includes only 23 selected papers presented at the Third Internnational Conference on Informetrics held during 9-12 August 1991 in Bangalore, to herald the Dr S R Ranganathan Birth Centenary clebrations. Includes one paper on Ranganathan's contribution to librametry. This is published in the 'Ranganathan Centenary Series', as Number 4.

RAVICHANDRA RAO, I K 319

Librametry to bibliometrics to informetrics.. Guest Editiorial, *Lib Sci slant Docum & Inf Std* 30 (2) June 1993: i-ii.

Traces history of bibliometrics which was called as librametry by Dr S R Ranganathan. Explains the scope of librametry and bibliometrics which suggests to examine the statistical distribution of documents. States that since mid 1980s this subject is popularly known as Informetrics. Mentions its scope and trends which is mostly towards discovery of theory and / or generalised mathematical model of library / information use phenomenon.

RAVICHANDRA RAO, I K and NEELAMEGHAN, A 320

From librametry to informetrics: An overview and Ranganathan's contributions, *Libri* 42 (3) July-Sept 1992: 242-257.

Traces the development of the application of quantitative mehods in library and informaion science. Discusses briefly contribuions of Ranganathan to quantification in library work and service, making the services more user-friendly and enhancing efficiency of library and informaion management.

SANGAM, S L 321

Librametrics, *DL*, 267-278.

Gives genesis of the term 'Librametry'. Gives its meaning and definition. Mentions scope of librametrics. Discusses application of the librametrics according to Ranganathan in the various areas of library and information activities. Concludes that librarmetric studies are a good indicator for measuring various activities of librarianship.

SEN, B K and TANEJA, RAM D 322

Confernece on informatics heralds Dr S R Ranganthan centenary year, *NISSAT Newsletter* 10 (3) July-Sept 1991: 20-21.

Reports about the Third International Conference on Informatics held in Bangalore during 9-12 August 1991 to mark the beginning of the Birth Centenary celebrations of Dr S R Ranganathan. Discusses about the Technical Sessions and Panel discussion.

SENGUPTA, I N 323

General introduction to librametrics and bibliometrics, *INICAE* 9 (2) Sept 1990: 191-205.

Elucidates librametry and bibliometry- two analogous and synonymous terms coined by S R Ranganathan and Pritchard. Discusses scope, application and development in India and abroad. Points out reasons for universal and restrcited accetptance of the two concepts. Presents general connotation and differences in their growth. Suggests ways and means to boost librametric research in India.

SENGUPTA, I N 324

Librametrics vis-a-vis bibliometrics, *IJILIS* 4(1) Jan-Mar 1991: 41-88.

Discusses two analogous or rather synonymous terms, librametry and bibliometry conined by S R Ranganathan and Pritchard respectively. Describes their scope, application and development including the reasons for the restricted/universal acceptance of these two terms.

SUBBA RAO, C V 325

Librametry case studies: science of measurement of library activities, resources and output phenomena, New Delhi; A B C Publishing House, 1992.

Deals with librametry as a tool to analyse library routines, work out staff formula, use of resources, users habits, etc. Traces the history of librametry. Advocates close association of statisticians with library and information scientists.

SUBRAMANIAN, R and NAVANEETHAN, R 326

Library Science with a slant to Documentation and Information Studies, 1981-1990: A bibliometric study, *Lib Sci slant Docum & Inf Std* 29 (3) Sept 1992: 157-162.

Discusses the various features of the issues of the *Library Science with a slant to Documentation and Information Studies* published during 1981-90. Indentifies the variations in content analysis which emphasises in information technology and quantitative studies, dominance of Indian authors, single authorship, etc. Suggests increase in volume of papers, review articles, research in progress, etc. to enhance the periodical's coverage.

TAHER, MOHAMED 327

Indian contribution to the field of bibliometrics, *Int Lib Move* 14 (2) June 1992: 79- 81.

Enumerates various writings in the field of bibliometrics contributed by Indian authors from Dr S R Ranganathan to date to highlight its development.

RANGANATHAN AND BIBLIOGRAPHIES

VENKATACHARI, P N 328

Ranganathan's views on Romanisation of Indian National Bibliography, *IASLIC Bull* 37 (3) Sept 1992: 183-185.

Traces the early years/phase of development of the Indian National Bibliography. Discusses that as INB had to cover publications in Indian languages and in Indian scripts, which are many, problems of romanisation were to be solved. Discusses views of Ranganathan in the matter obtained by the author.

WELLS, A J 329

Ranganathan's influence on bibliographic services, *SRR*, 11-13.

Describes briefly about Ranganathan's influence on bibliographical services, particularly in relation to indirect influence on Indian National Bibliography, British National Bibliogrphy, and others which used chain indexing of Ranganathan as a potential tool to derive subject headings.

REFERENCE AND INFORMATION SERVICES

ABDUL RAHMAN 330

Reference service in action, *Lib Sci slant Docum & Inf Std* 29 (3) Sept 1992: 148-156.

Discusses in detail the reference service in relation to the Five Laws of Library Science giving suitable examples from public libraries, sheding light on the catalogue room, reference librarian, etc, university library, industrial library. Provides suitable case studies wherever possible from these libraries. This is in honour of Dr S R Ranganathan, who loved reference service so much.

BANERJEE, MRINAL KANTI 331

Rererence service: Views of Dr Ranganathan, *RAT*, 38-43.

Explains the views of Dr S R Ranganathan on reference service with regard to Five Laws of LIbrary Science. Introduces the concept of short range reference service and long range reference service. Describes how information explosion and interdisciplinary research have created new techniques as current awareness service, selective dissemination of informaiton. Discusses Ranganathan's views about Natitonal Library also.

GOPINATH, M A 332

Humanising library and informatiton services: Role of the library profession, *Lib Sci slant Docum & Inf Std* 29 (4) Dec 1992: 203-212.

Analyses the factors that call for humanising the library and information activities. Identifies the various aspeects of information technology, information service, and information service that call for human knowledge. Presents Ranganathan's approach to these aspects of library service which is called Energising Library Service.

KUMAR, SUSEELA 333

From reference service to informatiton retrieval: Guest editorial, *Lib Sci slant Docum & Inf Std* 29 (4) Dec 1992: 165-168.

States that for Ranganathan reference service was the core of all library work. Mentions that with computers around it seems that machines will do it all but it is not true as human intervention will continue to be needed in new information technology. Gives advantages and disadvantages of computer, illustrating with manual and machine search studies. Concludes that no technology can beat the highly developed skill of information personnel who can analyse an information problem.

MOHANTA, RABINDRA NATH 334

Reference and documentation service in India's National Library: Present status and some proposals in the light of Dr S R Ranganathan's views, *RAT*, 30-37.

Defines reference service. Discusses its types as short range reference service and long range reference service. Defines documentation. Mentions its facets. Discusses doumentation service.Points out National Library as a documentation and bibliographic centre. Descriibes the present status of National Library with regrad to reference service, documentation service, reprographic service, special bibliographic service as printed catalogues. Suggests some proposals for National Library as user education programme, arrangement of reference collection, compilation of union catalogue, CAS, user's survey, etc.

RANGANATHAN, S R 335

Information service and imported confusion number one, *IASLIC Bull* 37 (3) Sept 1992: 107-117.

Reprinted from *IASLIC Bulletin* 2 (1-2) Dec 1957: 9-16, in view of its relevance, under the heading: 'Thus wrote Ranganathan'. Describes that information officers were appointed after independence without a clear understanding of their functions. Explains that information service presents, documentation service, aggressive reference service, precis service, and dissemination service necessary to increase industrial productivity. Wishes that library profession in India should excel and reach international level in research and service.

SEWA SINGH 336

From reference to information services: Impact of Ranganathan, *Timeless Fellowship* 15, 1993: 1-8.

Defines reference service. Gives developments of reference service. Describes the four categorisation of reference service, viz., initiation, general help to general readers, Ready reference service, and Long range reference service. Highlights Dr S R Ranganathan's unique contribution to reference service. Discusses its relationship with humanism. Presents analysis of reference work and service. Shows the symbiosis of reference service and classification. Concludes that Ranganathan was already out when the new technlology came in.

SEWA SINGH 337

From reference to information services: A study on impact of Ranganathan, *IASLIC Bull* 37 (3) Sept 1992: 171-176.

States that like everything else in library and information science, Ranganathan made a mark in reference service also, by putting forth novel ideas and actual case studies. Discusses development and categories of reference service into initiation, general help, ready reference and long range reference. Analyses mechanics of reference work and service to come up with a holistic view. Stresses upon humanistic side and symbiotic relationship with classification of knowledge. Disscusses that Ranganathan could not foresee the tremendous advancement in information technology to revolutionize all types of informtion service including reference.

SEWA SINGH 338

Ranganthan and refernece service, *CLIS Observer* 9 (1-2) Jan-June 1992: 16-22.

Discusses the concept of reference service as defined by S R Ranganathan in his writings. Traces the development of reference service. Gives various categories of reference service differentiating between the short range and long range reference services. Presents analysis of reference work and service as far as preparation, service and assimilatin are concerned. Gives Ranganathan's unique contribution to reference service from humanistic point of view, symbiosis of reference service and classification. Mentions relevence of Ranganathan's contribution in today's environs.

SEWA SINGH 339

Ranganathan and reference service, *DL*, 43-58.

Explain Ranganathan's contribution to reference service while giving its definition, development, categories, etc. Discusses relationship of reference service with humanism, classification, etc. Mention reference librarian and his flair. Describes the place of Ranganathan's reference service and its impact in the Western countries.

VISHWAMOHAN, V and CHANDRAMOHAN, V 340

Ranganathan and reference and information service, *DL*, 36-43.

Discusses S R Ranganthan's contribution to reference service giving its conceptual framework/ theoretical base. Points out achievement of post/s of reference librarian (s) in university libraries. Indentifies the items of literature Ranganathan published on reference service. Mentions about the moral strength and courage the fresh librarians receive from his words and deeds. Concludes that he had a great foresight about the new technology.

DOCUMENTATION SERVICES

KUMAR, P S G 341

Ranganathan's contribution to documentation, *DL*, 29-35.

Describes S R Ranganthan's contribution to the field of documentation in the demarcation of documentation activity into documentation work and documentation service. Mentions about the facets of documentation. Identifies the techniques of preparing various kinds of dicumentation lists. Discusses various documentation activities through such organizations as FID, Bureau of Indian Standards, INSDOC, DRTC. Gives the analysis of the concept and analogies of Ranganathan.

PARTHASARATHY, S 342

Ranganathan and documentation in India, *Jl Lib & Inf Sci* 17 (1) June 1992: 33-38.

Mentions S R Ranganathan as a builder of institutions. Describes his work/role in the formulation of standards for documentation. Gives background leading to the establishement of INSDOC, and DRTC. Concludes that the impact of Ranganathan on the development of documentation activities in India has been considerable.

DOCUMENTATION STANDARDS

GURCHARAN SINGH 343

Dr S R Ranganathan - images and echoes: Work on documentation standards, *Her Lib Sci* 32 (1-2) Jan-Apr 1993: 3-7.

Refers to the contribution of Ranganathan. Mentions entry of Ranganathan into library profession with no looking back. Discusses the work of Ranganathan in standardisation, formulation of national standards on documentation. Describes some personal traits of Ranganathan, his unbounded energy for dedicated work, his working pattern at the Indian Standards Institution (now BIS), his knack for involving others into work and setting his standards.

GURCHARAN SINGH 344

With Dr S R Ranganthan on standards for documentation, *Ann Lib Sci & Docum* 39 (2) June 1992: 38-45.

Mentions that Ranganathan gave the pioneer lead to the activity of developing and applying standards in India in documentation, information retreival, etc. Describes the infrastructure for standards. Discusses the role of Documentation

Sectional Committee under Dr Ranganathan and thus came the 'Evolution of Documentation' and the fourth standard of ISI was on the practice for make up of periodicals. Mentions about other standards also. Discusses some of the work qualities of Ranganathan as experienced by author.

PUBLIC LIBRARIES

NAVALANI, K 345

Ranganthan's dream, *RMM*, 116-120.

Points out the importance of rural library service. Describes how Dr S R Ranganathan pleaded for the development of rural library service as well as he did much for it. Explains how Ranganathan helped in the enactment of model public librararies act so that rural library service could be set up for the benefit of the masses.

PATIL, L M 346

Wanted : A public libraries network: Tribute to Dr S R Ranganathan, *Bhavan's Jl* 39 (20) May 31, 1993: 23-25.

Pays tribute to Dr S R Ranganathan in his Birth Centenary year. Describes his contribution particularly in getting the public library network which unfortunately could not be accomplished even after 46 years of independence. Makes an appeal to the Government of India to initiate uniform legislation for making public library services obligatroy.

PUBLIC LIBRARY System in West Bengal : 347

Ranganathan Birth Centenary Worksop, 11-13 September, 1992, Calcutta, organized by the Directorate of Library Services, Governement of West Bengal in collaboration with the RRRLF, Bengal Library Association and the West Bengal Public Library Employees Association.

Includes papers on four topics for the Workshop, namely 'Actual picture of the libraries in West Bengal...', 'Public Library service in West Bengal...' and 'The role of library in the movement of literacy, science and culture.

RAMAN NAIR, R 348

S R Ranganathan and the public library system, *Her Lib Sci* 32 (1-2) Jan Apr 1993: 21-29.

Discusses the work of Ranganathan in achieving functions and objectives of public libraries. Evaluates Model Public Library Act, 1930, model library bills and plans of Union Library Bill and library legislation in various states. Also discusses National Library Policy of 1986. Concludes that government should give priority to public library system lesgislation.

RANGANATHAN, S R 349

Philosophy of 'Free book service for all', *Lib Sci slant Docum & Inf Std* 29 (3) Sept 1992 : 119-126.

Reprinted from 'Free book service for all- an international survey' published in 1968. Defines the term 'All'. Gives the beginnings of free book service for all. Discusses social forces leading to free book service for all. Describes agencies for promotion of free book service for all. Mentions need for legislation for this commitment. Points out need for training of personnel to give such a service. Discusses the financial position for this purpose. Gives standards for viability.

RANGANATHAN, S R 350

Rural library service in the West, *In* Madras Library Association: *The library movement: A collection of essays by diverse hands*, Madras: MALA, 1929: Reprinted by Government Press, 1992, pp 122-124.

Discusses about the rural library service in the West that aims at providing literature to increase the value of school education, and its basis is the formation of a central collection of books. Talks about mobile library system also.

RANGANATHAN, S R 351

A typical municipal library of the West, *In* Madras Library Association: *The library movement: A collection of essays by diverse hands*, Madras: MALA, 1929: Reprinted by Government Press, 1992, pp 143-146.

Describes in detail the library system of a municipality of the West which consists of a central library and several branches and delivery stations. Mentions that a library has seven departments; lending, reference, magazine room, children, local collection, technical department.

TREHAN, G L 352

Public library movement and public library system-a dream conversation with Ranganathan, *In* G L Trehan and Girja Kumar: *Ranganathan Birth Centenary Monograph*, Chandigarh: Chandigarh Library Study Circle, 1993, pp 24-26.

Reports the conversation the author had with Dr S R Ranganathan at a night about the public library problems and setting up of an integrated system so as to provide efficient service, free of charges, to all.

PUBLIC LIBRARY / LIBRARY LEGISLATION

BISWAS, SDIT RANJAN and BALA KUMARI, N 353

Ranganathan's influence on library ligislation in India, *RAT*, 21-29.

Discusses need for and objectives of library legislation. Describes various efforts made by Ranganathan for framing of bills in the states. Explains library legislation in the states which have enacted them like Tamil Nadu, Andhra Pradesh, Karnataka, Maharashtra, West Bengal, Kerala, Haryana, and

Manipur. Discusses the present position of the states which have yet to enact library legislation.

JASMER SINGH 354

Impact of Ranganathan on public libray ligislation in India, *RMM*, 112-115.

Describes the cause of public libraries and library legislation Ranganathan took up soon after he entered librarianship. Mentions publications of Dr S R Ranganathan regarding public library act in India. Also mentions Ranganathan's last wish regarding enacting library legislation in India to set up nationwide network.

NAVALANI, K 355

The tallest torch bearer, *PP*, 117-122.

Explain about Ranganathan's interest in library movement and library legislation almost from the late 1920s. Describes about his efforts from 1933 which were largely unsuccessful, but he continued relentlessly to succeed in 1948. Discusses his passion for public library legislation and organised All India Seminar on Public Libraries in 1972 where he pleaded for National Grid of Public Library system for India.

PAHUJA, S L and GOYAL, S P 356

Ranganathan -an innovator of library legislation , *In* C P Vashisht (Ed), *Library movement and library development in India*: Seminar papers of Thirtyninth All India Library Conference, Dept of Public Libraries, Govt of Karnataka, Bangalore, January 7-10, 1994, Delhi: Indian Library Association, 1994, pp 156-159.

Describes the contribution of S R Ranganathan in the enactment of library legislation in four states of India. Traces his contribution from 1930 when he presented a draft Model Public Libraries Bill of India, and the subsequent draft bills. States that his ideas on library liegislation found full manifestation in the Mysore (Karnataka) Public Libraries Act.

RANGANATHAN, S R 357

Indian library manifesto, New Delhi: A B C Publishing House, 1990, 118 p.

Provides a blue print - a dream vision of author - for developing a National Grid of libraries for India. Contains all the papers of the author on library legislation, a subject so dear to Dr Ranganathan till his last days.Includes seven chapters with introduction by P N Kaula.

NATIONAL LIBRARIES

BANDYOPADHYAY, BALLARI 358

Ranganathan and role of the National Library, *RAT*, 16-20

Describes how Dr S R Ranganathan's recommedations in connection with the funcioning of the National Library have been made effective within the constraints of the system. Discusses about the various National Library services including the automated information services, reprographic services, information network by database communication.

HUMPHREY, K W 359

Ranganathan: National and university libraries, *RAW*, 42-49.

Brings out Ranganathan's contribution to National Library of India on the model of the former National Central Library, London. Refers to the suggestions made by Ranganathan for the NCL, London. Mentions about his point relating to the Copyright Library. Discusses Ranganathan'contribution to the setting up of university libraries, particlarly, with the reports he prepared for the University Grants Commission (India). He established various norms and standards which revolutionised the scence in Indian universities and colleges. Mentions about the education needed by the librarians.

SPECIAL LIBRARIES

NEELAMEGHAN, A 360

Information for small enterprises, Bangalore: Sarada Ranganathan Endowment for Library Science, 1992. 165p.

Aims at specialised training and guidance of information personnel to cater to the needs of the small and prospective enterprises. Brought out as the first publication of the newly started "Ranganathan Centenary Series", it pays rich ributes to Dr S R Ranganathan in his Birth Centenary Year.

SOUVENIRS ON RANGANATHAN

ALL INDIA Library Conference, Indian Library Association, 38th, Bhubaneswar, 21-24 November 1992, *Souvenir*, Department of Library & Information Science, Utkal University, 1992. 39 plus many unnumbered pages. 361

Brought out on the occasion of the 38th All India Library Conference of Indian Library Association, held at Utkal University, Bhubaneswar from 21 to 24 November, 1992 during the Birth Centenary celebrations of Dr S R Ranganathan. Includes some articles about library and information science education in Orissa.

CHANDIGARH LIBRARIANS' ASSOCIATION 362

Souvenir, Chandigarh: Chandigarh Librarians' Association. 1992. unnumbered pages.

Brought out to commemorate the Birth Centenary of Dr S R Ranganathan (1892-1972). Includes various articles, write ups and messages, about S R Ranganathan, his life, work and contribution, honours and awards, career, foriegn tours, etc.

IASLIC, 15th National conference, Annamalainagar, 26-29 December 1992. *Souvenir*, Annamalainagar: Annamalai University Library, Department of Liabrary and Information Science, 1992, unnumbered pages. 363

Published on the occasion of the Birth Centenary celebrations of Dr S R Ranganathan, the luminary in the field of library and information science, while organising the 15th IASLIC National Seminar hosted by Annamalai University Library and the Department of Library & Information Science.

INSTITUTE OF LIBRARY SCIENCE, HYDERABAD 364

Souvenir, edited by S Sudarshan Rao, Hyderabad: Institute of Library Science, 1991, unnumbered pages.

Dedicated to the memory of Dr S R Ranganathan, Father of Library Movement in India, during his Birth Centenary celebrations. Includes articles on libraries, library science education, library associations in Andhra Pradesh contributed by various authors in the field.

PUNJAB LIBRARY ASSOCIATION, PATIALA 365

Souvenir: Ranganathan Centenary celebrations, April 29-30, 1994 at Punjabi University, Patiala, Patiala: Punjab Library Association, 1994. 37 plus many unnumbered pages.

Published to mark the Birth Centenary celebrations of Dr S R Ranganathan, on the occasion of a Seminar organised by the Punjab Library Association on the theme: "Ranganathan: Man and his Mission", during 29-30 April, 1994. Includes articles, messages, etc about Dr S R Ranganathan.

SPECIAL NUMBERS OF JOURNALS ON RANGANATHAN PROFESSIONAL JOURNALS FOREIGN JOURNALS

INTERNATIONAL CLASSIFICATION, Vol 19, No 1, 1992. 366

A specialised journal in the field of library classification and knowledge organization, being published from Germany since 1974 under the editorship of Dr I Dahlberg. It has recently changed its title to "Knowledge Organization". It has published Volume 19, No 1, 1992, pp 1-62 as a Special Number devoted to the memory of Dr S R Ranganathan. Includes four papers from four countries on and about Ranganathan, besides an Editorial paying rich tributes to Ranganathan.

LIBRI: INTERNATIONAL LIBRARY REVIEW, Vol 42, No 3, July-Sept 1992. 367

It is being published from Copenhagen (Denmark) since 1951, and in which Dr S R Ranganathan published some of his early papers. *Libri* has brought out a Special Number, Volume 42, No 3 July-Sept 1992 under the invited Editorship of Prof A Neelameghan, a close associate of the great master. Besides the Editor's Introduction, there are eight papers written by experts from different countries including USA,Denmark, India, UK.

INFORMATION DOCUMENTATION,Vol 26, No 2, 1992. 368

It is published from Romania, and is brought out to commemorate the memory of Dr S R Ranganathan on the occasion of his Birth Centenay Celebrations world wide. Includes some articles, Editional on and about Ranganathan.

INFORMATION MANAGEMENT REPORT, August 1992. 369

It is published from the United Kingdom, and this Special Number has been published to pay tributes to Dr S R Ranganathan, the Father of Library Movement in India, on the occasion of his Birth Centenary celebrations all over the world.

LIBRARY TIMES INTERNATIONAL, Vol 9, No 1, July 1992. 370

Published from the USA, and edited by R N Sharma this July 1992 Number of this World News Digest of Library and Information Science, carries an Editiorial on Dr S R Ranganathan to pay tributes to this great world librarian on the occasion of his Birth Centenary celebrations. Also includes interviews with the new President of IFLA which organised 58th General Conference in New Delhi in August-September 1992.

BOLLETINO, AIB, Volume 32, No 4, December 1992. 371

This Special Number of this querterly journal contains three articles on the life and contributions of Dr S R Ranganathan whose Birth Centenary fell in 1992.

INDIAN JOURNALS

ANNALS OF LIBRARY SCIENCE AND DOCUMENTATION, Volume 39, No 2, June 1992: 372

This quarterly journal edited by JK Ahluwalia published a Special Number on Dr S R Ranganathan, who, incidently, was the founder of this Journal, way back in 1954. This Special Issue has been brought out in commemoration with the Birth Centenary celebrations of the stalwart of Indian librarianship, as well as a respected librarian and writer at the international level. Includes eight papers, besides an Editorial, by such friends and associates as Girja Kumar, A P Srivastava, T N Rajan, Gurcharan Singh, M A Gopinath, etc.

CLIS OBSERVER, Volume 9, Nos 1-2, January-June 1992 373

This Issue of this quarterly journal edited by D.R. Kalia includes only two articles about Ranganathan's contribution to the field of library and infomation science. Pays tribute to the great master on the occasion of his Birth Centenary Year being celebrated world wide.

COLLEGE LIBRARIES, Volume 8, Nos 1-2, 1992. 374

This Special Number has been brought out as Dr S R Ranganathan Commemoration Volume, by the West Bengal College Libraries Association, Calcutta. It contains eight messages, an editorial, and a few words from the Convener. Besides, it has included seven articles on the life and words of Dr S R Ranganathan. Pays homage to this great teacher and organiser of Library Science. However, all the authors of this Special Issue are from the state of West Bengal only.

DESIDOC BULLETIN OF INFORMATION TECHNOLOGY, Volume 12, No 5, September 1992. 375

This Special Number of this Bulletin of Defence Scientific Information and Documentation Centre, Delhi, has been brought out as Dr S R Ranganathan Birth Centenary Issue. Includes five articles on Ranganathan's life, career and contribution by the authors from within the country as tribute to this exemplary teacher and apostle of librarianship. Includes also a brief but well written Edtorial about Ranganathan's contribution.

HERALD OF LIBRARY SCIENCE, Volume 32,Nos 1-2, January - April, 1993. 376

This Issue edited by P N Kaula has been published as a Special Ranganathan Centerary Number as a tribute to him in his Birth Centenary year celebration. Dr S R Ranganathan has been a regular contributor to this quarterly journal being published since 1962 first from Banaras and now from Lucknow. It includes three photobraphs of Dr S R Ranganathan, and covers 13 articles written by library and information professionals from all over the country including two from abroad (Denmark and USA). The articles touch some episodes from his life, career, and professional contributions. The Editor has contributed three articles on different aspects of Ranganathan including Centenary literature.

IASLIC BULLETIN, Volume 37, No 3, September 1992: 97 -243, Edited by S K Kapoor and Subir K Sen. 377

Brings out a Special Number as "S R Ranganathan Birth Centenary Commemorative Issue". This is the only Special Number which includes three articles by Ranganathan himself published earlier in the same journal. Besides this, includes eight more articles by the various authors from across the country. Another special feature of this Special Issue is that it includes three sets of letters of Ranganathan written and received by him. It also covers book reviews of some of the books published on Ranganathan in 1992. Includes a well written `Introduction' by Subir K Sen about the Special Number.

IJILIS NEWS LETTER, 1992, Cuttack. 378

Brought out as a Special Issue of this *Newsletter* marking salutations to the Father of Library Science in India on his 101st birthday. Reports about the various celebrations organised in the country on the occasion of Ranganathan Birth Centenary. Publishes a photograph of Padmashree S R Ranganathan on the title page.

INDIAN JOURNAL OF INFORMATION LIBRARY & SOCIETY, Volume 5, Nos 3-4, July-December 1992, Edited by B B Shukla. 379

Brought out as a Special Number on Ranganathan Centenary and Orissa Library Movement, with a photograph of Ranganathan, giving its salutations to him . Edited by B B Shukla, this issue includes three articles on the life, and contribution of Ranganathan by four Indian authors. Pays tribute to the Father of Library Movement in India in the year of his Birth Centenary celebrations.

INDIAN BOOK CHRONICLE, 1992 380

It has brought out a Special Issue on Dr S R Ranganathan to commemorate his Birth Centenary Year (1992) by publishing book reviews of such books as were written on him to mark the occasion.

INDIAN BOOK INDUSTRY, Volume 45, No 2, 1992. 381

Published as a Special Issue on Dr S R Ranganathan, Father of Library Movement in india, to commemorate his Birth Centenary Year by publishing book reviews of such books as were published on him during 1992 to mark the occasion.

JOURNAL OF LIBRARY AND INFORMATION SCIENCE, Volume 17, No 2, December 1992, Edited by Krishan Kumar. 382

This six monthly journal of the Department of Library and Information Science, University of Delhi, has published a Special Issue to mark the Birth Centenary celebrations of Dr S R Ranganathan who established this Department way back in 1947-48. Includes articles on the life and work of S R Ranganathan by his close friends, his students and associates, thereby paying tributes to the great luminary in the field of library and information science, when international conferences are being held all over to mark the occasion. Its December 1992 Issue also contains an article on S R Ranganathan's contributions to library classification.

LIBRARY HISTORY REVIEW, Volume 3 No 4, 1992. 383

This quarterly journal from a private publisher, based at Calcutta, carries only one article in its Volume 3, No 4, December 1992 on Dr S R Ranganathan as a token of tribute to this great Indian library scientist and Father of Library Movement, on the occasion of his Birth Centenary Year.

LIBRARY SCIENCE WITH A SLANT TO DOCUMENTATION AND INFORMATION STUDIES, Volume 29, No 2, June 1992 384

Devoted to documentation and information studies, this quarterly journal founded by Dr S R Ranganathan himself in 1964 is now published by the Sarada Ranganathan Endowment for Library Science, Bangalore. It brought out a Special Number Volume 29, No 2 June 1992, dedicated to Dr S R Ranganathan on his birth centenary.

It carries a Guest Editorial on Ranganathan by S Parthasarathy (of the Institute of Information Studies, Madras); a summary of the work and achievements of Ranganathan by M A Gopinath; and seven more articles by Indian and foreign authors. This journal has also published its Volume 29, No 3, September 1992 as Special Number on Dr S R Ranganathan as it carries a Guest Editorial on Ranganathan by M A Gopinath, one article by Ranganathan himself, a couple of more related articles, and a Ranganathan Birth Centenary report. The No 4 for December 1992 of the same Volume also carries one article on Ranganathan as well as Reports of the 58th IFLA General Conference and Second International ISKO Conference, held to commemorate the Birth Centenary of Dr Ranganathan.

LIBRARY TODAY, Volume 14, No 9, Septmber 1992. 385

This monthly library periodical is published by the Andhra Pradesh Public Library Association, Hyderabad, contains two articles on the life and works of Dr S R Ranganathan in commemoration with Centenary Year falling in 1992, and celebrated world wide.

LUCKNOW LIBRARIAN, Volume 24, Nos 1-4, 1992. 386

This quarterly journal published by the U P Library Association, Lucknow published on all the four Numbers of Volume 24 for 1992, a photograph of Dr S R Ranganathan as a mark of respect and tribute of him during the Birth Centenary celebrations being celebrated the world over.

NISSAT NEWSLETTER, Volume 11, Nos 1-4, 1992. 387

This quarterly *Newsletter* of the National Information System in Science and Technology, Department of Scientific and Industrial Research, Government of India, New Delhi, carried on all its four Numbers a coloured photograph of Dr S R Ranganathan, the Father of Library Movement in India. Also it reported from time to time about the Birth Centenary celebrated in various insitutions in the country and elsewhere.

TIMELESS FELLOWSHIP: Annual Journal of Library and Information Science, Volume 15, 1993. 388

It is published as an Annual from the Library and Information Science Association, Karnataka University, Dharwad. In its Volume 15, 1993, it carries an article on Ranganathan and his contribution to the development of reference service, a library service so dear to him.

NON-PROFESSIONAL JOURNALS

BHAVAN'S JOURNAL, Volume 39, No 20
May 31, 1993. 389

This non-professional journal has published a Special Number, Volume 39, No 20, May 31, 1993, dedicated to the memory of Dr S R Ranganathan. Published by Bhartiya Vidya Bhavan, Bombay, this Special Issue carried a coloured photograph of Dr S R Ranganathan on the cover of the Journal, and includes three articles on the life and works of Dr Ranganathan.

FRONTLINE, Vol 9, No 17, August 15-28, 1992. 390

This fortnightly magazine published by Kasturi & Sons, Madras, has published four articles including one on S R Ranganathan, the library scientist and father of the Colon Classification, marking his Birth Centenary celebrations. The other three articles and write-ups are on different aspects of libraries and library science.

UNIVERSITY NEWS, Volume 30, No 35, August 31, 1992.
Editor: Sutinder Singh. 391

Although this has been brought out as a Special Issue on University Libraries in order to present a state of the art report of the university libraries in India, yet it carries a photograph of Padamshri S R Ranganathan on the title cover, and two articles on Ranganathan's life and work and a Centennial assessment reviewing Ranganathan's autobiogrphy, as a tribute on his Birth Centenary. It was released on the occasion of the 58th IFLA General Conference held during 30 August - 5 September 1992 in New Delhi. Includes an Editorial 'A moment for reflecion' about Ranganathan's life, career, achievements, and contribtions.

NEWES PAPERS

THE HINDU, August 30, Madras, Sunday, 1992 392

This famous and more than a century old daily news paper published from Madras and some other places, brought out a Special Supplement on Libraries and Dr S R Ranganathan, and distributed free to the participants on the opening day of the 58th IFLA General Conference, held in New Delhi during 30 Aug - 5 Sept 1992 to mark the Birth Centenary celebrations of Dr S R Ranganathan.

PART - II

SUPPLEMENT

LIFE AND WORK, BIOGRAPHY

BALACHANDRAN PILLAI, S 393

Dr S R Ranganathan: The father of library movement in India, *In* Raman Nair, R (Ed), *Public library development*, New Delhi: Ess Ess Publications, 1993, pp - 1-5.

Discusses about the life and work of Ranganathan, his education, his career at different places, his library tour abroad, contribution in setting up of INSDOC and DRTC. Describes his role in developing public library system in India, the books and articles wrote, formulation of Five Laws of Library Science, development plans for libraries, the prizes, awards and acknowledgements he received for his contribution to library and information science. States that Sayers called his period 'The Age of Ranganathan'.

GANAPATHY, V 394

Father of library science in India, *In* Ravi, N (Ed), *The Hindu speaks on libraries*, Madras: Kasturilal & Sons, 1992, pp 278-279.

Deals with the birth, early education, professional training, appointments, work and contribution of Dr S R Ranganathan whose Birth Centenary celebrations are being celebrated at Thanjavur District Library. Discribes his achievements and recognitions he received in India and abroad. Discusses about the special meeting organised by Thanjavur District Library to launch the Centenary celebrations of the doyen of library science.

GUPTA, K BALASUNDARA 395

Father of library science, *In* Ravi, N (Ed), *The Hindu speaks on libraries*, Madras: Kasturilal & Sons, 1992, pp 280-281.

Describes the work and contribution of Dr S R Ranganathan who invented Colon Classification which earned him international fame. Discusses about his other contribution as PMEST, Classified Catalogue Code, Five Laws, and many more. Mentions about the places he worked and the awards and honours he received from abroad.

RAJAN, T N 396

The relevance of Dr Ranganathan's ideas 396 in the information age, *Ann Lib Sci & Docum* 39 (2) June 1992: 31-33.

Examines briefly the relevance of Ranganathan's ideas and contributions in the present context of information age. Cites implications of his Five Laws and interprets their value in the present day information handling problems. Lists a few areas for the application of his methodology of subject structuring. Mentions ground work for library routines as analogous to algorithms for computer programming and analysis for PERT/CPM. Suggests that his ideas are valid even today for serious study.

RANGANATHAN, S R 397

Memorabilia Ranganathan, edited by M A Gopinath, Bangalore: Sarda Ranganathan Endowment for Library Science, 1994. xiii, 83 p.

Attempts to make live the thoughts of Prof S R Ranganathan who was a thinker, analyser, consolidator of his thoughts and used to put them in a crisp and telling manner; the thoughts ranged on many subjects, but most of them were on library and information services. States that this forms part of Ranganathan Birth Centenary Celebrations. Contains a short biography of Ranganathan in the beginning, and also includes source documents for quotations. Besides, it includes 17 chapters on various aspects of libraries, library services, library education, etc.

SHARMA, R N 398

Ranganathan: A world librarian; Editiorial, *Library Times International* 9 (1) July 1992: 14.

Describes about the birth, education, career opportunities, and the literature Ranganathan produced which made him ultimately a librarian; and he got recognition from around the globe for his novel ideas in librarianship.

SHARMA, R N 399

Ranganathan: A world librarian, *In* P P Rawat and S R Gupta (Eds), *Kaula festschrift volume*, 1994.

Explains in detail the work and contribution of seminal value done by S R Ranganathan in the field of library and information science that he ultimately came to be known as World Librarian, and received many international awards, honours, degrees by way of recognition.

COMPARATIVE BIOGRAPHY

BARUA, P 400

Prof P N Kaula: A legacy of Dr Ranganathan, *In* P P Rawat and S R Gupta (Eds), *Kaula festschrift volume*, 1994.

Describes about the life and works of Prof P N Kaula during his professional career. Explains in detail how Kaula has been influenced by the devotion, dedication to work for the cause of libraries and library services. Describes Kaula as the legacy of prof S R Ranganathan.

KUMAR, P S G 401

Ranganathan and Kaula: Paradoxical linkages, *In* P P Rawat and S R Gupta (Eds), *Kaula festschrift volume*, 1994.

Presents an analysis of the work of Prof P N Kaula and that of Prof S R Ranganathan pointing out a clear impact of Ranganathan on Kaula as librarian, teacher, editor, project designer, and so on. While explaining the paradoxical linkages between the two, mentions about the work P N Kaula did for Ranganathan during his life time and even after him in popularising his ideas.

THILLAINAYAGAM, V 402

Kaula: A true disciple of S R Ranganathan, *In* P P Rawat and S R Gupta (Eds), *Kaula festschrift volume*, 1994.

Discusses about the impact of Dr S R Ranganathan on Prof P N Kaula in every respect, particularly the way he has become a crusador of the cause of library service all over the country and abroad. States that how Kaula has been contributing to the body of literature, preaching the ideals of Ranganathan, the great master wanted to be emulated by the professionals. Concludes that P N Kaula is a true disciple of Prof S R Ranganathan.

RANGANATHAN DICTIONARY

VENKATAPPAIAH, V and KUMAR P S G, *Eds* 403

Ranganathan dicitionary: Indian library and information science, New Delhi: B R Publishing House, 1994. viii, 116 p.

Lists the library and information science teminology coined, defined, elaborated and used by Dr S R Ranganthan. This is a compendium of the Indian school of thought of library and information science.

RANGANATHAN AND LIBRARIANSHIP

DEVARAI, RAJASHEKHAR S and DAMODARAM,T 404

Ranganathan and the professional development of librarians: study in professiology, *Univ News* 30 (45) Nov 9,1992: 11-13.

Discusses about S R Ranganathan's achievements, honours and awards, professional image and status. Describes librarianship as a profession. Explains Ranganathan's vision, approach and the professional model, while describing his volumious contribution of 60 books and 2000 articles. Highlights the legacy of Ranganathan which is far advanced and ahead of our times, especially as far as philosophy and theory of library and information science are concerned; concludes with the best tribute to him and his inspiring prayer.

COLLECTION DEVELOPMENT

SHAKUNTHALA, K A 405

Collection development, Ranganathan's APUPA Pattern and resource sharing, *In*, IASLIC, *Collection development in the context of economic recession*: Papers, XIX All India Conference of IASLIC, 26-29 December 1993, Birla Institute of Technology Mesra, Ranchi, Calcutta: IASLIC, 1993, pp 13-14.

Discusses about Ranganathan's expalanation of the arrangements of books and other library collection. Looks at the entire problem of transformation and mapping from the point of view of reader in context of the APUPA Pattern. States that resource sharing will be the best ideal for librarians, and collection development policies be developed using Ranganathan's APUPA Pattern.

LIBRARY CLASSIFICATION

CIGANIK, MAREK 406

Modular faceted marker passing in textual data, *Lib Sci slant Docum & Inf Std.* 29 (1) Mar 1992: 32-40.

Outlines the problem of the automatic text analysis. The starting point is Ranganathan's full title creation and analysis, which is very important for national bibliographic system. Elaborates the faceted marker passing theory. Gives implementation on meta-informational base with modular construction. Applies information flow principle in a semantic network- like structure based on information nuclei of Fundamental Categories formulated as a complex semantic relational model of text.

GOPINATH, M A 407

Creativity and knowledge organisation: A cognitive interaction, *In* A Neelameghan, and others (Eds), *Cognitive paradigms in knowledge organisation*, Bangalore: Sarada Ranganathan Endowment for Library Science, 1992, pp 390-400.

States that creativity is a complex of processes of active thinking. It guides a mind to intuitively comprehend sublimated knowledge and intellectually analyse, synthesise, disseminate knowledge which helps problem solving. To be productive, knowledge resulting from such processes have to be cumulated into systems. Gives features of knowledge organisation. Discusses role of classification as a thread of knowledge, and classification provides a structure for learning. Concludes that knowledge of classification enhances the productivity of a creative person. Points out S R Ranganathan's productivity in this regard.

UMARANI, ASHA 408

Knowledge classification: A permanent structure for dynamic knowledge, *In* A Neelameghan, and others (Eds), *Cognitive paradigms inknowledge organisation*, Bangalore: Sarada Ranganathan Endowment for Library Science, 1992, pp 211-222.

Explains that a true library classification system came into being with the publication of Dewey Decimal Classification followed by many more schemes and an elaborate theory. Mentions about Ranganathan's contribution of analytico- synthetic scheme which resolved many issues, growth of knowledge after Ward War II changed the framework of knowledge, leading to the rejection of theory and turning to word indexing for information retrieval and further rejection of classification schemes when computers came. Discusses that Ranganathan tried but could not find the basis for dividing the universe of knowledge into main divisions comprising the first array; a problem which remains to be solved, though he did some home work in CC-7 also.

BIBLIOMETRICS. INFORMETRICS

RAVICHANDRA RAO, I K 409

A breif report of the Third Internationnal Conference on Informetrics, 9-12 August,1991, *In* - I K Ravichandra Rao (Ed), *Informetrics - 91: Selected papers* from the Third International Conference on Informetrics, Bangalore: Sarada Ranaganathan Endowment for Library Science, 1992,pp 547-575.

Reports about the Third International Conference on Informetrics held in Bangalore to herald the Birth Centenary Celebrations of Dr S R Ranganathan in which more than 100 delegates from about 14 countries participated. Mentions that it was inaugurated by A Neelameghan, Keynote address by A Bookstein, welcome by I K Ravichandra Rao and vote of thanks from G Bhattacharyya. Reports about the

Technical Sessions in which selected 32 papers were presented and discussed. The Panel discussion included F W Lancaster, Bluma Peritz, S Parthasarathy, Susan Bonzi with M A Gopinath as moderator. Appends a list of 102 participants and the programme also.

RAVICHANDRA RAO, I K 410

Welcome address, *In* I K Ravichandra Rao (Ed), *Informetrics - 91: Selected papers* from the Third International Conference on Informetrics, Bangalore: Sarda Ranganathan Endowment for Library Science, 1992, pp 1-8.

Welcomes the delegates from different countries including India to the Third International Conference on Informetrics held during 9-12 August, 1991 in Bangalore, as a part of the Centenary Year programme of the late Dr S R Ranganathan, an eminent librarian, teacher, and Father of Library Movement in India, and who coined the most meaningful term 'Librametry' for the first time in 1948 at ASLIB meeting in England.

PUBLIC LIBRARIES

RAMAN NAIR, R, *Ed* 411

Public library development, New Delhi: Ess Ess Publications, 1993, xi, 178 p.

This is published as Dr S R Ranganathan Centernary Volume for the remembrance of his contribution to the development of public library system in India. Includes 16 articles on different aspects of public library system including one article on the life and work Dr S R Ranganathan who earned fame at the international level because of his valuable contribution to library and information science.

SCHOOL LIBRARIES

DEVARAJAN, G and RAJAN, A C, *Eds* 412

Role of libraries in education, New Delhi: Beacon Books, 1994. xii, 181 p.

This is brought out as a commemoration volume to Dr S R Ranganathan, the doyen of Library Science, in his Birth Centenary year. Contains 15 articles on school librarianship covering different facts such as collection building, reading interests, user education, and so on. Brought out by the Kerala Library Association of the three-day seminar it organised in February 1992, where 21 papers were received for presentation. Includes the main recommendations made at the seminar.

PART - II

INDEXES

SUBJECT INDEX

AUTHOR INDEX